If You're Over 50
YOU ARE THE TARGET!

Rosemary K. Breckler

Bristol Publishing Enterprises, Inc.
San Leandro, California

Printed in the United States of America.

ISBN 1-55867-020-3

Cover design by Frank Paredes

TABLE OF CONTENTS

*To Daniel Wayne Lasater,
my wonderful son-in-law, and my daughter
Melinda, who so patiently shared him
when I needed him to iron out a
computer problem while writing this book.*

Introduction

There is no fiction in this book. I quote from an experience of my own or that of a friend, a relative, an acquaintance, from an interview or a reference. Information has been gathered from research and from my private files of years as a private investigator and a journalist.

My research was aided by reading the F.B.I. files on *Crime In America*. Ronald E. Warthen, Chief Investigator, Fraud Bureau, State of California Department of Insurance, who was a colleague of mine when I was a P.I., assisted me with information about staged automobile accidents by loaning me video tapes from their crime lab.

The television newsroom at Station KRON Channel 4, San Francisco, answered my questions and furnished me with information. Several departments of the San Jose Police Department offered me assistance, as did Better Business Bureaus from communities on the San Francisco peninsula and U.S. Government publications departments.

During the six months I spent writing this book, it seemed to me that scam stories proliferated like maggots in rotten garbage. I had to select only part of those that I felt would warn mature people to be on the lookout. In most cases I have disguised the true identities of the people I have written about and the location of their mishaps.

I sincerely believe that for every scam I uncovered, there are millions of happy satisfied people under the care of honest, sincere professionals in every field that I reported.

In spite of my warnings and revelations, I still believe in the innate goodness of most people and sincerity of American citizens no matter what their origins — and that most professional people are to be trusted.

1

HOW TO AVOID
GETTING FLEECED

Call it what you choose — sham, scam, swindle, fraud — it is all larceny and has existed from the beginning of recorded history. The definition of fraud is: larceny by trick. So it is the tricksters we are going to prepare to outwit at their own games in this book.

These tricksters, according to official estimates by the North American Securities Association, are responsible for losses from investment fraud in the United States totaling more than $40 billion a year. That doesn't count the hundreds of thousands of scams in other fields. Medicare, as you will learn in a later chapter, is a jackpot for swindlers.

But swindlers are everywhere, in every field, and can look as honest as a preacher, which in some cases is exactly what they are. Worse, it seems that almost everyone is a sucker — or "mooch" as con artists call their victims — at some time in their lives.

Victims have included doctors, lawyers, NFL football players, the elderly, yuppies, celebrities and politicians. Counting the people who have been victims of scams is almost equal to taking the census!

What makes it much harder to control in the 90s

is that since thieves must use ever more sophisti-
cated and organized methods to stay ahead of crime
prevention, the computer is becoming the crime of
choice.

But the old-style hustlers and con artists are still out
there plying their trade. In fact, the field is getting so
crowded that almost everyone can expect to be
scammed several times a year in some way or other.

ARE YOU SOMEONE'S SCORE?

While the average person is busy going about life,
con artists are constantly sizing people up for their
most vulnerable points of attack. And they have
found that the easiest sheep to shear are:

- very busy affluent people
- happy relaxed vacationers
- weak kindly elderly people

But this list is only the beginning. Confidence
games may victimize bereaved people by reporting
that a deceased person has ordered merchandise.
You could be betting your life when you get taken
by a health fraud scheme. Salespeople often make
exaggerated claims for products or services they are
selling, such as roof spraying that will prolong the
life of your roof for ten years. Watch out for high-
yield investments and pyramid-type schemes —
someone always gets cheated on these illegal plans.

How do they do it? It is the experience of fraud investigators that all con artists rely on three human
motivations to defraud their victims.

Greed: Greed resides in almost all of us. We can't resist a "good deal" or getting something for nothing. Someone has said that we all have a little vein of larceny built into us. Some examples of con games that rely on greed are investment schemes, "pigeon drops" and fencing operations. Convincing you that you can get rich at home is also a common scam.

Goodness: Most of us love to help other people, especially someone with a sad story to tell. Examples of con tricks that prey on your kindness are phony charities and door-to-door sales, especially if they help "the underprivileged."

One example of a con which is spreading across the country is the shabbily dressed man or woman who stands near a busy shopping center, looking very pathetic, while hopefully holding aloft a sign that reads in very large letters: *Will Work For Food.*

Frequently the sign holder doesn't want work. He wants you to feel guilty for being able to spend at the shopping center while others go hungry. He wants you to stop just long enough to give him money. Some have been known to receive $500 a day for this scam.

Gullibility: This is the net that catches the most fish. We like to believe that people are truthful and this trust gets us into trouble. Even con men get conned by other con men! Repair persons tell us we need unnecessary parts. So do some inspectors. We are easily deceived by complicated wording in contracts and believe the salesperson when he or she says it's "just a standard sales contract — you don't need to really read it."

A CON MAN'S VIEW OF YOU

To see inside a swindler's mind, read these two quotes:

"I was a con. We don't mind robbing and injuring people as long as it benefits us. We see people as prey." Quoted from a letter to the editor, published September 1990 in a national magazine, written by a con artist now serving 15 years in a penitentiary.

Another con artist, his face camouflaged, paroled after serving three vacations on the state for bilking people out of many thousands of dollars, told a television interviewer, "You don't understand, do you? It's a game! You like to play the horses? You like the odds in blackjack? The risk is exciting. And, your odds are a heck of a lot better than they are at Vegas. I never thought of them as people! They were just marks. When you play poker, do you feel sorry for the cards if you win?"

So now we know. We are all sheep someone may someday fleece. What to do? This book hopes to enlighten you enough to make yourself less vulnerable. It can serve as a road map, with all the good roads, bad roads, detours and roundabouts pointed out to you.

HIGH TECH LARCENY

Larceny has grown with the years. In the very old days bankers locked their vaults with a key. Robbers learned to pick locks. So combination locks were invented. Thieves ground out the locks. Then combination locks were made from metal that couldn't be ground out, so they found minute creases in the vaults, inserted nitroglycerine and blew up the vaults.

Vaults were then constructed with no cracks or creases in them anywhere, so the crooks kidnapped the bank president to open the combination lock. Time locks were installed that even presidents could not open. Swindlers then turned to computer fraud via automatic teller machines and are now trying to penetrate electronically transmitted funds.

But this book is going to concentrate on fraud down at the individual level where it affects all of us and hurts the most. We all have to learn to be ever more on the alert because fraud rates have increased much faster than larceny.

In the past 20 years, fraud arrests have grown from 146% per 1,000 population in the U.S. and Canada to 264% by 1986 and steadily rising. In comparison, larceny has grown from 118% to 123%. The difference is because fraud is easier than theft by stealth. Losses from credit cards, for instance, have increased 50% in the last five years.

Since computers were often used in these scams, it must be noted that by 1990 one computer was owned for every 50 people in the United States.

Offenders arrested for fraud crimes are older and better educated. In 1985, the median age of a swindler in Canada was 31.9 and in the U.S. 31.5. Only a few decades back most criminals had "retired" by the time they were 25. Now we are confronted by criminals well over age 60.

SCAMS COME UNDER MANY CATEGORIES

financial planners	brokers
rare coin dealers	limited partnerships
land swindles	travel gyps
gold investments	other rare metals
commodities	campsite memberships
new and used cars	weight reduction
insurance	medical treatments
telemarketing	plastic surgery
movers	contractors
repair services	charity collections
credit cards	love and romance
switch and baits	mail orders
C.O.D.s	and many more

There is always a new plan developing, each a fancy title for a swindle!

CAN YOU RECOGNIZE A CON ARTIST?

Con artists and thieves are very upset if they suspect they are being seen through! They make a hasty exit.

Most con artists talk very fast, change the subject often, rarely make eye contact, make it hard for you to follow the conversation closely, even use double talk that leaves your mind reeling. They confuse you to make you more vulnerable.

They usually "have your number" before they make the pitch. They even keep sucker lists! If you've been taken once on an investment scam, you can expect to be taken again.

They are constantly studying people, looking for easy marks. At this very second someone somewhere is analyzing you or some of your records. Maybe for good reasons, if you have just applied for a loan or a mortgage; maybe not.

They may be checking to see how many credit cards you have. How active are they? In other words, how much money do you owe? The more cards you have and the more money you owe, the better the opportunity to tap into your credit without detection.

New privacy laws are being enacted to protect your credit records and personal life, but they have a long way to go before they stop the information which has been collected for good reasons from getting into the hands of the wrong people.

Unfortunately, these new privacy laws can also work against you. These same safeguards can make it impossible for you to locate a business manager, consultant, investment counselor — whatever he called himself — who just bilked you out of, say, $10,000. The laws are his shield.

SCAMS HURT YOUR SELF-ESTEEM

When you discover that you have been "taken," you really suffer. Feeling like a fool doesn't build up anyone's self esteem. You just know that you should have been brighter, more on the ball.

Numerous reports reveal that when people who feel they should have known better get taken in any racket, usually they sheepishly swallow their losses and bruised self-esteem.

Scam artists know this. They count on the victims to keep their ill adventures to themselves. The victims may never make the same mistake again. But since they don't pass the word, the games go on and more people become victims.

YOU MAY NEVER KNOW

There are many scams, some so small that you never even suspect that you have been scammed.

For instance, at a huge chain supermarket near my home after 8:30 P.M. on a Sunday night, my neighbors stopped in shock and observed the man in the meat department carefully remove all the stickers from the packages of leftover meat and apply fresh stickers with the next day's date. Neither this couple nor I have purchased meat at that store since.

Another friend bought new draperies for her living room and family room. Her husband said, "The price was obscene!" A check of the yardage actually used (by measuring the length of each outside seam and the width of the bottom hems), compared with the amount of yardage stated on the bill, disclosed that they had paid for twice as much yardage as they got. They called in another drapery man, got his estimate of yardage needed and then went to Small Claims Court. Their money was refunded before the case came to court.

Expect rip-offs everywhere you shop. Pay attention to the size of the currency you pay with — don't let the cashier tell you it was a ten when you know it was a twenty! Carry as little cash as possible. It is easier to return bad purchases made with a credit card. Count your change. Study your sales slip. Items purchased on sale sometimes are charged at the regular price. An item can be repeated on a sales slip when only one was bought.

If you must daydream or meditate, do it at home, alone, or in your own garden! This is the route to financial survival!

Faulty merchandise, returned for credit, is sold as new. Unneeded repairs are made at great prices. "Inspectors" gain access to homes. Phoney "payment due" bills are mailed to short-handed offices. Widows are induced to sign loans on their houses that they have no way of repaying.

The goal of this book may sound familiar. It is the motto of the Boy Scouts of America. *Be Prepared!* If you are, you may never have to live with the grief and the loss from being ripped off by a clever crook.

2

WHO'S THAT PEEKING THROUGH YOUR KEYHOLE?

Our lives — through computers, laser full-color copiers, cameras that can take pictures in the dark, voice-activated tape recorders, and computer programmed telephones — have become very transparent.

Someone out to study you can peer into almost any one of your records. In spite of fighting to preserve our privacy, there is very little of it left.

For instance, every month your telephone bill lists the numbers you have called. By using a reverse directory which all newspapers, law enforcement agencies, and many other people own, someone can look up who you called and find out what kind of business you phoned.

Your credit card bills give records of where you shopped. The check you pay your bills with tells where you bank. The checks you deposit reveal where you earn your money. Your checking account reveals where you live. Your neighborhood speaks many words about you.

The car that you drive, the restaurants where you eat, the clothing that you buy, any purchase that you have made since the era of computers are all tattle-tales!

If you buy a number of vacation items all at once and then charge plane or cruise tickets, it is possible for peeping Toms to know where you have gone and how long you will be gone.

THE SECRETS YOU GIVE AWAY

Have you ever stopped to think how many of these records you have given away? Was it always necessary to fill out all the forms? Answer all the questions? Whose business is your life, besides your own? What does it have to do with warranties on toasters?

Many times you give access to your life and your bank account without even knowing it. You lay yourself wide open every time you order merchandise over the telephone, charge it to your credit card, give your telephone number and address.

True, most of the employees in these companies can be trusted. But frequently they are low paid and shift jobs often out of boredom. There is no way to be sure they won't carry your information with them when they leave. Or sell it to some scam artist.

Shopping from television or catalogs may be a convenience you enjoy. But is it worth the risk? Do you want that many eyes able to peek at your financial records? Someone can use your charge number to order things by phone for himself. Or sell your card information to someone else. Either way, the items will be on your bill after the culprit has disappeared.

Lazer color copiers can photograph your checks and your signature so well, even banks have trouble recognizing the difference. Your signature is retained, but the payee and amount are altered. You can protect yourself by always writing your check and signing your name on anything with a pen that uses light blue ink — it doesn't copy well. For this same reason, when ordering by mail or telephone it is better to send a check written with light blue ink, than it is to charge it to your credit card. The delay will be minimal.

WHO'S THAT LISTENING IN ON YOU?

There are men and women who do nothing, all day long and most of the night, except drive slowly through affluent neighborhoods. They report by cellular telephone to a tape recorder in an office.

They can listen to any conversation going on in the neighborhood over a cordless telephone. They can hear everything that is going on inside a house with a "baby monitor" in use. They can eavesdrop on car telephones within one half mile of them. They can hear a husband explaining what time he will be home for dinner! Or Mom and Dad advising the babysitter how late they will be.

All of these conveniences use radio waves. If you must broadcast on them, don't discuss business or personal affairs. Most important, avoid mentioning your address, or times and places that you will be away from your home.

14

WHO'S THAT SPYING ON YOU?

Sometimes the car's occupants are studying houses for the best time to break into them. Sometimes the driver of the car is getting a "make" on a specific person. Maybe the habits of a woman he wants to rape. Or perhaps he is planning a kidnapping. Sending out messages over radio phones is like the old poem, "I shot an arrow into the air. It came to earth, I know not where!"

Someone could be checking to see which radio station or television programs you favor. It might be the FBI. Securities Exchange Commission. Police. Or a private investigator. But whoever it is — whatever their reason — our lives have become houses of glass.

RESEARCHING YOUR BUSINESS

It doesn't stop with surveillance of our houses. Every level of our lives can be researched.

In this country there are three major credit bureaus which will furnish information on any of us, to anyone who inquires for it, in some cases pays for it, without our being informed that this information has been acquired, by whom, or why.

When you apply for a mortgage it has become standard practice for the bank or loan company to require that you furnish copies of the first pages of your federal income tax returns for two or three previous years to establish your income. This becomes public property. The mortgage can be sold or traded to another firm; your records go along with it. And yet, *it is illegal for the IRS to reveal this information* which bankers demand of you.

There are large organizations in this country that do nothing but amass information about you: what kind of moral character do you have? What magazines do you read? What is your level of income? What kind of neighborhood do you live in? Who are your kin? What is your employment potential? What kind of grades did you get in which schools? Where and when do you like to vacation?

Companies make a good income gathering information for the benefit of insurance companies: your living habits, the dates, medical treatments, chronic ailments you have had treated where and by whom, the times you have sued or been sued.

The University of Illinois recently conducted a survey and discovered that approximately 42 percent of Fortune 500 companies collect secret personal data on their employees. This is information collection on a big, big scale.

Any of this information, for a price, can be sent by fax machine, computer or telephone across the country in moments, to anyone who inquires. Con artists at the big money level have never had it so easy!

3

HOW DO SCAM ARTISTS MEASURE YOU?

Not too long ago a middle-aged couple arrived in New York carrying a nondescript briefcase. They were a jeweler and his wife; the briefcase was loaded with the most valuable gems from his New England jewelry store. They wanted to sell them at the Jewelry Mart, close their business and retire.

As they walked slowly through the airport, two men approached and one said, "Sir, you're losing money." They kept on walking. The other man followed them and handed them several coins.

"There's money falling out of your pockets." The woman looked worried.

"Have you got a hole in your pocket?" she asked her husband. He shook his head and kept walking.

One of the men touched him on his shoulder and handed him folded up dollar bills.

"What's a'matta? You got money to burn?"

At this point the jeweler was very concerned. He let go of his briefcase for a second to feel his pockets — and the briefcase was gone!

How did the scam artists know the jeweler and his wife were carrying valuables? The couple gave themselves away. They were too tense. The jeweler held the briefcase too tightly. The wife walked too close beside him like she was guarding the briefcase. They didn't talk to each other. They looked around anxiously from the corners of their eyes. The shabby briefcase didn't go with the nice clothes they were wearing.

A GOOD TARGET IS EASY TO FIND

It is unfortunate that in order to sell magazine and newspaper advertising and get subscribers, publications frequently publish demographics. In addition, there are magazines and journals that specialize in demographics.

Information is shown in colorful pies, graphs, or lists. Where are the most affluent areas in the country? Are the people white collar, blue collar? How many people over a certain age are in what income bracket? Where have they retired? What was their lifestyle before they retired and what is it like now? What are their hobbies? Do they live off interest, pensions, or hold post-retirement jobs?

Graphs are also published showing exactly how and where retirees from different areas and states invest their money.

You can even purchase computer programs, in color, that show demographics, including the wealthiest retirement areas. Some of these maps will be divided up into colors: dark green for the billionaires; sky blue for the next wealthiest; yellow for the next in line; on down to the pink regions where affluent professionals retire on pensions.

UNNECESSARY HEART BYPASSES TOP THE LIST

Joseph Giordano, M.D., director of the Center for Vascular Disease at George Washington University Hospital in Washington, DC, claims many bypasses performed were unnecessary and other treatments less remunerative to the physicians would have worked.

Dr. Giordano, better known as the surgeon who saved former President Reagan's life after Reagan was shot in a 1981 assassination attempt, recently stated, "There are too many people undergoing bypass surgery when they could do just as well by reducing risk factors, by exercising, and by just waiting out the first signs of vascular disease."

As far as the older population is concerned, he says there also are too many vascular diagnostic procedures being done. In too many cases, he claims, the tests are ordered simply because Medicare covers the costs.

The booklet *Heart Attacks* contains facts about this number one cause of death in the U.S. It includes major causes of heart disease, methods of treatment, and how you can reduce the risk. You can obtain this government printed booklet No. 132W by mailing $1.00 to:

R. Woods
Consumer Information Center-P
P.O. Box 1001
Pueblo, CO 81002

It is always recommended that no surgery of any kind be performed without at least three surgical opinions; that is, from three doctors who are not connected by self interests. *All surgery puts a patient's life at risk.* Or, runs a chance of making the condition worse.

Each one of these abuses of both the patient and Medicare puts Medicare in greater jeopardy, and the sheer number of them, coupled with the cost, starts rumblings between generations. Tampering with Medicare scams the working generations as well as the retired generation.

UNNEEDED CATARACT SURGERY FRAUDS

A physician in my area opened an eye center with a partner in 1986. His services included cataract surgery, lens implants and radial keratotomy.

Cataracts are a clouding of the eye's lens, which causes blurry vision. To treat the problem, eye surgeons remove the lens from inside the front of the eye and slip a plastic lens into its place.

In the case of the physician arrested for performing unneeded cataract surgery, elderly people were invited to come to his eye center for a free eye exam.

A center van picked them up and drove them to the clinic. After the doctor examined their eyes, he said they had cataracts, and he scheduled surgery for a few days later.

State investigators, armed with patients' medical records, looked into numerous complaints. They immediately took five elderly men and women, scheduled for cataract surgery, to independent ophthalmologists, who all agreed that not one of these people required cataract surgery.

A man, about to turn 90 but with eyesight good enough that he passed his California driver's licensing test on the first try, and his slightly younger wife, can't recall how he was contacted by the physician or why he made the appointment. But they both could see well enough to read and watch television.

On the day of the appointment the man didn't need to drive. A van pulled up to the couple's home and they were driven to the eye center, where the doctor told them they both needed their cataracts removed as soon as possible and scheduled surgery for a few days later.

But the medical board already had an "eye" on this eye doctor. An investigator took the couple for a second opinion. No cataract surgery was prescribed.

One 86-year old woman was very upset by her fading vision. She had gone to a number of doctors, all of whom told her she suffered from macular degeneration, a condition in which the retina degenerates. However, when she went to this same eye clinic, the doctor told her she had cataracts and recommended immediate surgery, which he promised would restore her vision.

Her son, however, wasn't convinced. He took her to a few more doctors who all said she had macular degeneration and declared that a cataract operation would accomplish nothing. He filed the complaint with the medical board.

The medical board then filed five charges against the doctor, involving five men and women, ages 76 to 91, who allegedly were told by the doctor they needed unnecessary cataract surgery. Other ophthalmologists testified that the surgery was not called for in these cases.

HEALTH CARE PRODUCTS

During the 90s you can expect health care products to be the biggest scams in the medical field. Among them are:

overpriced vitamins	water purifiers
bogus arthritis remedies	weight-loss plans
baldness remedies	nutrition schemes

Door-to-door salesmen, television and magazine ads will promise that most of these products, once you are using them, will qualify for full payment by Medicare (if you are a Medicare recipient) as soon as your doctor signs the forms stating that they improved your health. This is frequently not the case! You get stuck with the bill and the item often turns out to be useless.

Start first by discussing the need with your doctor. If you belong to a health maintenance plan, they may have free classes or literature on these subjects. But why are you talking to the door-to-door salesman in the first place? That's a big *no-no* to safeguard yourself from scams. If you are lonely, call a friend, or talk to a neighbor.

AIDS SCAMS ARE THE CRUELEST OF ALL

Whenever there is an epidemic of any kind, the scam worms crawl out from under the rotting logs which they use as hideouts and rush to sell their "wonder" products to the most desperate. The rise of the AIDS epidemic has not failed to catch their attention.

Authorities have reported that these predatory quacks are offering such things as a "vaccine" produced by culturing AIDS patients' urine, thus removing the virus from the urine, and once it is "purified," then injecting the urine back into the patient.

They offer pills, too. These are called *T-cells* and the shams claim that these pills will increase the number of AIDS-fighting cells in the body's immune system. An investigator for the new California AIDS Fraud Task Force, which is headed by the state's deputy attorney general, has analyzed them and claims they are nothing but sugar pills.

Other fraudulent products sold as anti-AIDS treatments include snake venom, algae, hydrogen-peroxide injections, herbs, the food preservative BHT, and various preparations claiming to boost the body's immune system, including tea made from the bark of a Brazilian tree.

While some AIDS sufferers fear that government intervention may stifle development of alternative treatments that may have merit, most authorities are worried about what they consider to be pure exploitation of AIDS victims by quacks and promoters.

Because of all the fraudulent products sold as treatment for AIDS, the attorney general's office formed the Task Force, a loose-knit coalition of two dozen experts from law enforcement, health and regulatory agencies, to investigate the dozens of wily schemes that keep preying on "the desperation of those with AIDS, those who have tested positive for the virus, or on the fears and ignorance of the general population."

One of the biggest hurdles that needs to be crossed to make this task force successful is overcoming the reluctance of AIDS victims to reveal that they have been taken in by a fraudulent product.

But the con men never seem to run out of ideas. The most extremely dangerous cure that they sell consists of hydrogen peroxide to be taken orally or by injection. According to a deputy city attorney in San Diego, "The poison control people say this caustic solution releases such large amounts of oxygen that it burns the throat and virtually explodes in the bloodstream."

An ozone machine that supposedly "oxygenates" the blood and can cost hundreds of thousands of dollars is another of their scams. So are coffee enemas and herbal concoctions.

To prey upon the fears of those who do not have AIDS, disinfectant sprays are offered for telephone receivers as well as super toilet seat covers. Health authorities point out that no one has ever contacted AIDS from a telephone or a toilet seat.

The U.S. Postal Service, by challenging ads for AIDS cures that are handled through the mail, has succeeded in removing 15 out of 16 from the mails.

HOME EMERGENCY RESPONSE SYSTEM FRAUDS

Another hoax designed to ring every penny out of an older person is the sale of some kinds of home emergency response equipment. If you live alone and have frail health you are bound to be on a calling list.

You are also hustled with television scare commercials telling you how your life could be saved or helped if only you install one of these systems in your home.

"All you need is the little red button to wear around your neck and disabled older people like yourself need never worry about calling 911 or anyone else for help. Just press the button and help will be rushed to you. The price is only $300, which includes installation and hookup at your hospital or the police or their service. . ." or so the commercial rants.

The television quacks who frighten you with this commercial and misrepresentation are the worst kind of con artists, out to rob the feeblest people.

Or maybe the salesman who talks to you will charge even more. Thousands of elderly people fall for it every month somewhere in this country. Such systems are advertised in magazines, on television, on your telephone and by salesmen who come to your door.

The salesman and the commercials tell you they are selling you a "guardian angel," and "How can you put a price on such a service? It can save your life!" Often they will high pressure you with scare tactics, confusing you into signing a contract.

A survey of people over 50 who responded to these frightening television commercials reported that when the salesman called on them, the equipment installation costs were quoted as high as $3,000 to $5,000 and on top of that there were monthly charges of $30 to $90 — with all sales final. If the system is no longer needed, or wanted, it cannot be returned.

Yes, emergency response equipment can save your life, but such systems can commonly be found in hospitals, offered at substantially lower prices. These systems are rented from the hospital and can be returned at any time when they are no longer needed.

Depending on which hospital you rent from, and the type of equipment you choose, installation charges will cost you less than $100 and you can expect monthly fees to be less than $50.

If you are ill, disabled, or have a worrisome condition, talk it over with your physician. Then shop around. Prices differ even within small areas. The smallest price will still get you exactly the same service!

If you purchase a unit through the mail, and then discover that you could have rented an inexpensive unit from a hospital, in many states you have a right to cancel the order within three days. Usually the salesman who comes to your door just takes your order and your check and the order is handled further by mail. In this circumstance you would qualify for a full refund.

But the safest thing to do is always to say, "I need to talk this over with (my son, doctor, or name anyone). Could you please call me back tomorrow or could I call you?" You can expect to hear, "But this offer is a special! It's only good on my first visit. Then the price is higher."

Translated, that means "I get two-thirds of the price as commission."

Be firm. "I'll just have to take a chance on that." Guide him to the door. (Why did you admit him in the first place?) Or hang up the telephone. Then check with your doctor or hospital!

HEARING AIDS WHETHER YOU NEED THEM OR NOT

Among these 90s scams are free hearing tests by hearing aid manufacturers, sometimes in vans sent to senior centers, sometimes at grocery stores and shopping malls, sometimes offered in ads. Almost everyone over the age of 50 suffers some loss of hearing for high frequency sounds. But if you can hear normal conversation and everything else that you need to hear, you don't need a hearing aid. Even if you are missing parts of conversation, for some types of hearing loss, the hearing aid being pitched to you may not help you, and perhaps *no* hearing aid will make appreciable difference.

Medicare is billed more than $250,000 a year for providing people with hearing aids which will not help them. And the victims have to shell out for them too, sometimes the entire amount, because their doctors refuse to be unethical and sign the form saying the hearing aid was needed.

If you suspect you're not hearing as well as you should be, go to an accredited (and in some states licensed) audiologist. He (or she) is qualified to give you an in-depth hearing assessment. He will refer you to a physician if he suspects that you need medical treatment. He will also assess your hearing with a variety of hearing aids, and recommend that you purchase the aid that gives you the best possible results. He has no affiliation with hearing aid manufacturers.

LITTLE MACHINES THAT "KILL" PAIN

There is a small machine called a transcutaneous electrical nerve stimulator (TENS) that looks like a transistor radio, worn on a belt around your waist, developed to reduce pain. Sometimes it works. Sometimes it doesn't.

It is advertised as absolutely "free" to you, as Medicare pays the bill if you are old enough for

Medicare. But many times physicians will not authorize the item and the victim ends up paying the full $500.

CHAIRS THAT LIFT YOUR BANK ACCOUNT

The same goes for "seat lift chairs" heavily advertised on television and in magazines. Medicare more and more often is refusing to pay for these expensive pieces of furniture which often do not serve the purpose as well as using a cane to arise from a chair. Guess who gets stuck with the bill?

One woman watched such a chair being advertised on television, called the number only for information, and found the chair delivered to her living room within three hours.

The fast-talking salesman who accompanied the delivery man told her, "All you have to do is get your doctor to sign an authorization form stating you needed it and it has improved your condition; then Medicare will reimburse you for it."

Other items promising to be great helps that Medicare may *or may not* pay for:

- bed and wheelchair cushions
- skin care equipment
- three-wheel powered carts which have been known to tip over and injure patients

YOU'RE DRINKING SWAMP BILGE!

How many people have been revolted over that announcement and at the sight of the vial of murky water the salesman has just held up to them *that he drew from their faucet?*

They forget that they have been drinking this water for a long time and not been made ill by it. They don't stop to think that maybe he already had something inside the vial to make the water become murky. They hear only the conclusive proof spoken to them by the well-rehearsed salesman.

Incidently, this salesman arrived in the house by leaving a card hanging on the front doorknob.

"The water in your neighborhood is suspect," it read. "Several of your neighbors have had us test their water. If you would like a *free test*, call this number."

The call was made, and he came running with his kit so fast that you would think he was a fireman and their house was on fire.

When the man arrived, he pulled some chemicals out of his testing bag and ran some tap water into a bottle. All the while he was talking rapidly.

"Lots of stuff gets down into the water. Pesticides, fertilizers, cleaning fluids, used oil — you never know what you are drinking unless it is tested."

Sure enough, the water in the vial he used turned murky. He shook his head in sympathy.

He had a fast answer prepared for any question. After a some seconds he added a few drops of an unnamed chemical to the water. Within a few minutes a sludge-like residue formed at the bottom of the bottle.

"That swamp bilge," he made a face, "is what you are drinking!"

His scare tactics included: "Government standards are not stringent enough. The sludge at the bottom of the vial can make you sick. The white calcium spots on your glasses and dishes can give you kidneystones and painful calcium build-up in your joints."

But this homeowner asked for time to think it over before shelling out $4,000 for a system to purify his water. The next day he took his own sample, in a clean glass jar, to an independent lab. The water tested out to be well within both U.S. and state health standards in every respect.

He learned that the "sludge" produced in the bottom of the vial by the added chemicals was really only dissolved solids including calcium, magnesium and iron, which aren't even among the minerals regulated as primary contaminants that endanger health.

Doctors disputed the kidney stone claim. "As long as you're urinating, you're getting rid of any calcium," a urologist informed the homeowner, who still has the $4,000 safely in his savings account.

FOR CANCER CURES, ONLY THE BEST CLINICS

Swindlers have a dozen different cures to offer you, all explained in their best golden voices. But your best chances of survival still lie with treatment at the most reputable clinics.

Quacks usually have you travel somewhere to take

treatments which have not yet been recognized or even discovered by the U.S. Board of Health or the American Medical Association or revealed in the New England Journal of Medicine.

But never fear: all you have to do is pay their fee, then take a plane or drive across the border and they will cure you miraculously. There are two problems with these unapproved cures. In many cases they kill or maim and in all cases they give false hope which, when dashed, can lead to mental depression and suicide.

Have you ever met anyone, heard someone interviewed on television, or seen anyone who had been cured by one of these wonderful cancer remedies? Wrack your brain and you will only be able to refer to hearsay. In the meantime, desperate people are casting hard-earned dollars into the laps of these smooth-tongued quacks.

ARTHRITIS CURES ABOUND

After cancer comes arthritis. More than $400 million a year is spent on harmful treatments and devices. Cures are very rare.

Take the copper bracelet, as a small example. This amulet promises to relieve, even cure arthritis pain. Are you wearing one? Or has anyone you've known worn one? Did they ever report that it accomplished anything except being a nuisance on their wrist?

5

SHOULD YOU DOUBT YOUR DOCTOR?

More and more people are beginning to realize that all doctors are not gods, delivering medical care because they are concerned about their patients' welfare. The vast majority of doctors are faithful to their profession, but the truth has to be faced — there are con artists in doctors' smocks, too.

IS HE REALLY WHAT HE CLAIMS?

Be careful when you pick a "specialist" on your own. Even though a physician is listed as a specialist in the Yellow Pages, it may mean only that he is *practicing* in a special area, not that he has taken special *training.*

A study published in the *New England Journal of Medicine* (regarded as the most authoritative in the country) found that 12 percent of specialists listed in the phone book are not board-certified to practice the specialty that they attribute to themselves.

You should always verify this before you make an appointment with a doctor. You can call the doctor's office and ask if the doctor is board-certified, and if so, in what specialty. You can also ask which hospitals he works in and check with them.

HOSPITAL BILLS

You should know that it is always very important to check your hospital bill thoroughly, just as you do your credit card purchases and hotel bills.

A problem common enough to warrant exposure on a national news broadcast recently is double billing by hospitals. For example, you're being billed for an appendectomy. At the top of the bill, it tells you that the procedure is $2450. Under that cost, the bill is itemized: so much for pharmacy, so much for surgery, so much for hospital room, so much for anesthesiology. And then *the figures are added to the initial amount*, thereby doubling the cost of the appendectomy!

A study conducted by a major life insurance company found that hospitals overcharge by an average of $998 on bills over $10,000. Make sure you received the services you were charged for. And if Medicare is paying the bill, do yourself a future favor by reporting the error to Medicare. It can help to safeguard the future of Medicare.

WHO OWNS THE LABORATORY?

In the state of California, "referral scams" have lately been much in the news. These relate to laboratories, hospitals, and speciality clinics which are owned by physicians. The physician in question refers a patient to a health care business in which he himself is an investor or co-owner.

This tempts the physician to order all kinds of unnecessary and expensive procedures, which causes a chain reaction. It defrauds Medicare, Medicaid, and the patient, creates unnecessary fear and pain for the patient, disrupts lives. Some medical procedures can even cause maiming or death.

California State Representative Pete Stark, D-Hayward, claims that this practice is a scam that barely evades federal anti-kickback laws. He stated that these referrals are nothing but "scams designed to influence doctors to illegally refer patients and that *these partnerships are being used to buy and sell patients.*"

Dr. Arnold S. Relman, editor-in-chief of the esteemed *New England Journal of Medicine*, claims, "Joint ventures increase costs and cause unnecessary duplication of services because hospitals spin off only their most profitable services and promote them heavily."

The American College of Surgeons has decided it is "an unethical conflict of interest for doctors to refer patients to facilities in which they are investors."

Dr. Lee F. Rogers, chairman of the American College of Radiologists, told Congress in September 1990 that they used to allow the practice but stopped it four years ago because, "They found that the potential for, and actual abuse and exploitation of patients by unethical practices and the flagrant disregard of physicians' responsibilities to the patient were too great and too pervasive under these arrangements and therefore could not be ignored."

A federal study in 1989 found that patients of doctors who owned medical labs got 45 percent more lab tests than other patients. Other studies showed that the problem was much more severe in California, which was the most lenient on the practice.

This is why it is so important to find out if your doctor is a partner in any medical facility he refers you to. He shouldn't require a double return from serving you. His profession is physician, not scalper.

And you shouldn't have to endure unnecessary anxiety, pain and inconvenience. Or, if your insurance doesn't pay the entire bill, you shouldn't have to pay this unnecessary expense.

HOW DOES YOUR DOCTOR RATE?

While most scamming by doctors is related to insurance companies and Medicare, there are some doctors who give such shoddy service that you are risking your life by putting your health in their care.

Because "these dangerous doctors who fall through the cracks continue to kill, maim, defraud and otherwise injure their unknowing patients," consumer advocates have formed the Public Citizen Health Research Group.

For this reason more and more doctors are being disciplined, and their names and ratings are being published so you can be aware of who to avoid.

This consumer advocate group has put together a two-inch thick roster in a state-by-state form which lists actions that have been taken against 6,892 medical professionals who have been disciplined by state and federal agencies. It covers 40 states and the District of Columbia.

"If your doctor is among the 6,892 on this list, you ought at least to question the quality of his or her care," suggests Dr. Sidney Wolfe, director of the Public Citizen Health Research Group. "At the very minimum, you should find out why he is on the list."

He points out that the nation's system for protecting the public from incompetent physicians has vastly improved in the last 15 years, but remains inadequate. The group was founded by consumer activist Ralph Nader.

He claims that gaps in medical data on medical professions "snake all across the landscape." Therefore the guide contains the names of physicians, dentists, chiropractors and podiatrists who have been disciplined by state medical boards, Medicare or the U.S. Drug Enforcement Administration.

Also, each state's section lists doctors who have addresses in that state but were disciplined by medical boards in other states. It also contains the reason for the action, where available.

Public Citizen asked state medical boards and federal agencies for actions taken against doctors since 1985. Some states provided actions that went back even further, while others provided data for only the last year or two.

State medical boards in Alabama, Alaska, Colorado, Oklahoma and South Dakota *adamantly refused* to reveal any wrong-doing by their medical professionals.

Five other states — Arizona, Arkansas, Maine, Mississippi and New Mexico — were willing to provide at least some information, but for various reasons did not.

Copies of the guide may be ordered from:

> Public Citizen Health Research Group
> Department QD
> 2000 P St. N.W.
> Washington, DC 20036

The cost is $30 for individual consumers, consumer groups and government agencies; $100 for businesses, doctors and lawyers.

HOW DO YOU CHOOSE A DOCTOR?

With people moving around the country so much for business and pleasure reasons or retirement, there often comes a time when you need to choose a new doctor. How do you go about it?

If you are new in a community, your former doctor may have a good referral for you. You can also ask your local hospitals or your county medical society to give you a list of referrals. Most of these referrals will offer internists, family physicians and some specialists.

In most medium-sized or large cities where there is a university medical center located, the medical center will provide physician referral services. Many large university hospitals offer outpatient-referral services. Nurses at these large institutions can use a computerized data base to locate the names of physicians who might fit your need.

If your problem is specific, you might try calling or

It therefore takes years for a doctor to be competent enough to perform this surgery. Yet doctors, with no experience except from what they have read or seen, have attempted face lifts!

Why risk a doctor who hasn't been highly recommended by friends who have used him? Face lifts aren't secrets any longer — women, and sometimes men, discuss them openly.

LIPOSUCTION

The nation's most popular cosmetic surgery currently is liposuction, because fat that is suctioned off stays off. Again, there are no guarantees.

Liposuction allows a surgeon to "sculpt" the human body; it relies on a machine rather than on good diet or exercise habits to rid the body of stubborn fat.

In the search for the Body Beautiful, liposuction promises the ultimate: a chance to get something for practically nothing. It is hard on the surgeon and risky for the patient.

To be the most successful, the antifat assault requires a patient who is already of nearly normal weight. It is discouraged for obsese patients, because it can often require blood transfusions and carries higher risks.

Even in the most skilled hands, liposuction is a crude operation, which requires brute strength to force a metal tube through hard fat. The cosmetic results are hard to predict.

Any medical doctor with absolutely no training in

this technique can set himself up as a specialist. This is because there is no specialty certification required to practice liposuction. Experience as a plastic surgeon is not required.

This leaves the door wide open for all kinds of scams. The price of one procedure is from $1,500 to $4,000. One treatment can remove four pounds of fat at most. A doctor can buy the suction machine for $4,000.

Congressman Ron Wyden of Oregon, who has held hearings on cosmetic surgery fraud and abuse, said, "A cosmetic surgeon can buy equipment Monday morning, do two procedures Monday afternoon, and make money all day Tuesday."

Besides the fast and huge profit, liposuction is attractive to greedy doctors because it is so casually regulated. All liposuctions are performed in doctor's offices. This eliminates a most important quality control step: hospital privileges, given only to surgeons whose peers consider them qualified. The offices of bogus liposuction practitioners do not need to be accredited.

A doctor must undergo almost ten years of study and training after medical school graduation to be certified in plastic surgery. A board certified cosmetic surgeon must have completed five years of extra study and training after he received his M.D. and pass a two-day test.

Complications. During each liposuction treatment the doctor forces a long, blunt instrument far into the patient's body, jarring and rocking loose the deep-seated fat cells. Nine out of ten patients, mostly women, can expect to be sore and bruised for six weeks or more and can experience pain, swelling, numbness, and pigmentation discoloration. These are the successes!

The worst risks may be danger of muscle damage, bowel performation, and death. During each treatment as the fat is extracted, body fluids rush in the fill the tunnel. Life-threatening fat or blood clots can develop in these tunnels. If the blood clots travel to the lung or brain, it can be fatal.

By August 1989, eleven deaths had occurred.

Final results. If all goes well, trusting you used a good plastic surgeon, you can wear a dress several sizes smaller. But your beach wardrobe may have to be designed to cover scars.

In some women the skin heals in unsightly ways — wavy, baggy, lopsided or splotchy. Thigh and buttock liposuction will leave excess skin that may not shrink to fit.

Since you will risk so much, suffer so much pain and pay so much money, why not use the best surgeon you can locate?

- Check out his certification.
- Ask whether a hospital gives him surgical privileges.
- Check with that hospital.
- Check with the local library or the Medical Association to see what the medical training is

for a person with his certification.

CELLULITE!

This word has haunted, even ruined, the lives of some women. Beauty scammers have frightened, shamed, tortured women into believing cellulite, the little cottage cheese type dimples that appear in the skin of thighs and buttocks, must be destroyed at all costs.

Nicole Ronsard coined the word *cellulite*, a non-medical term, in France and introduced it into the U.S. through her best-selling book. Ever since, women have spent hours and fortunes trying to remove this perfectly normal condition that is not fat deposits. Neither is it caused by laziness, aging, over-eating or childbirth. Girls as young as ten years old sometimes have cellulite.

No amount of steaming, rolling, wrapping, pounding, massaging, dieting, exercising can remove it, because it is not fat, but spaces. The exact cause is still a mystery to medical science.

Cellulite consists of fibrous bands that go from the connecting tissue that covers the muscle to tie up to the skin. Some of these bands are shorter than others and cause a kind of puckering of the skin.

Some doctors, not plastic surgeons, now practice cellulite reduction. They use a forked instrument with rounded tips and a cutting edge at its center, which catches and severs the fibers that are causing the dimpled skin. The doctor makes many passes with this instrument, in a radiating pattern, before injecting the patient's own fat, removed by liposuction. Since tissue drapes when the patient is lying down, the patient must stand during the long, tedius, painful procedure.

Since scarring occurs, patients cannot always wear the sports attire or bathing suits they may desire.

As in other plastic, cosmetic and liposuction surgeries, complications have occurred. Inexperienced, noncertified doctors are attempting cellulite reduction treatments and this poses additional risks to the patient. Before you trust your body to any doctor, check him out! (See Chapter 5, page 37.)

RETIN-A SCAMS SCAR FOR LIFE!

All kinds of fake Retin-A creams have flooded the market, advertised as over-the-counter products. They are in drug stores in all parts of the country. The trouble is that these fakes do not, cannot, contain tretoin, the ingredient that can be sold by prescription only and the ingredient that makes the cream work!

The scam products can actually increase wrinkling. Some can permanently discolor the skin. Some are sold in drug stores under the drug store's brand name. Many are promoted by pharmacists who are the sole, or part owners of the cream manufacturing company.

Even if you use the real thing, prescribed by your doctor, you are in for some disappointments. Retin-A tends to lose its value after it has been used over a long period of time. If you use these wrinkle-reducing creams, you must never, never go out in the sunshine again without a very large hat or a veil. Forget about your Caribbean cruises or Hawaiian vacations unless you intend to stay under cover.

Retin-A horror stories may help you to think twice about this "miracle" cream.

- One woman forgot to tell her beautician she was using it and had an eyebrow waxing. When the wax came off, so did the top layer of skin.

- Another user was having her eyelashes and eyebrows dyed when a drop of dye dribbled on her skin. In trying to remove it, the cosmetician rubbed a raw spot that was slow to heal.

- Without thinking, one user put a drop of perfume on her neck. The skin became deeply discolored, like a birthmark. It took a long time to fade.

- Some users found that their skin became very thin and fragile, looked too smooth like they'd had a bad burn, and was far too shiny always.

The FDA has never approved Retin-A as an anti-wrinkle cream. Its sole recommended purpose is for treatment of acne in adolescents. For these reasons, the interest in Retin-A is slowly fading.

PERMANENT MAKEUP MEANS FOREVER

The latest fad, tattooing your makeup on forever, means just that. You don't need to waste time each morning putting on lip outlines, eyeliner, eyelashes, eyebrow pencil. But what the nymphs are forgetting is that forever is forever.

If a woman ages gracefully, her hair and makeup tones should become softer, which makes her look more lovely. This means black eyelashes, eyebrows and eyeliner should fade to light tan and that ruby lips that begged to be kissed in your youth look sweeter in pink in your mature years.

But tattooing is forever. And sometimes while tattooing the eye liner, eyes have been damaged. Serious bacterial infections also have occurred.

Tatooing makeup on is not a scam, but it's a risky business. Almost anyone can set himself up as a tattoo artist. There is no protection for the customer and the business attracts fly-by-night operators. No license is required in most states.

So what if you can sleep an extra ten minutes in the morning. Forever is a lot longer than ten minutes! Especially if the person you allow to tatoo you makes a serious error!

COLLAGEN

Save your money and do not buy collagen facial creams. Regardless of claims to the contrary, collagen, a protein made from the hides of cows, has a structure too coarse to be absorbed by human skin, and therefore *cannot* change the condition of your skin. And for some people, it causes a violent allergic reaction.

Collagen is used, however, to inject into lips, producing the popular "bee stung" lips cherished by models and actresses, and into frown lines and other facial lines to plump them up.

The procedures costs from $300 to $600 and must be repeated every three to six months, depending on how long it takes the body to absorb the collagen.

Although there have been few reported side effects, doctors and nondoctors, even nurses and beauticians, are getting into the business. If the injecting needle isn't sterile, it can cost you your life. Don't risk this procedure unless you go to a qualified physician.

BREAST ENHANCEMENTS

The American Society of Plastic and Reconstructive Surgeons, which represents America's board certified plastic surgeons, has issued the warning: the use of fat transplants for breast augmentation is extremely hazardous.

The breast procedure is unsafe, says the American Society of Plastic and Reconstructive Surgeons, because much of the injected fat cells will die and form scars. This will make early detection of breast cancer difficult. Disease may go undiscovered, or false positive mammography and xerography results may produce increased breast biopsies for benign conditions.

popular that you frequently saw people nibbling on chunks of cheese they carried in pockets or purses. In spite of all the protein they devoured, they grew tired and anemic. They did lose weight. But after awhile they were in the doctor's office for treatment. The remedy turned out to be pasta, fresh vegetables and fruit. All the things they had been avoiding.

But make up a new diet, put it in a book, get it published, and hopeful converts will chase you across the country wanting to get on your bandwagon, even if your diet consists of cow manure mixed with rotten eggs.

Some have tried getting their jaws wired shut. People are occasionally seen with staples in their ears. About 20 years ago people were having part of their intestines removed so they wouldn't absorb so much from their food.

At a friend's house one night, I met a woman who had recently had her intestines tied off. Several years later I encountered her again. She had regained her weight and now suffered from painful scarring and adhesions as a result of the surgery.

All these methods confirm one truth: *you can't lose weight without exercising and cutting down on your food intake while eating a balanced diet.*

When Nancy Wellman, American Dietetic Association president, testified before a congressional subcommittee investigating the weight-loss industry, she stated that rapid weight loss is advised "only for dieters who are at least 30 to 40 percent over-weight."

"Even then," she said, "it should be undertaken only with the supervision of a qualified health team, including a physician and registered dietitian."

WARNING!

Because dieting has become not just a national fad but almost a frantic epidemic, the National Council Against Health Fraud warns dieters to avoid commercial weight loss programs that:

- promise rapid weight loss, defined as substantially more than one percent of total body weight per week.
- promote diets below 800 calories a day unless under medical supervision. Diets of 1,200 calories are preferred.
- misrepresent sales people as "counselors" supposedly qualified to give advice in nutrition and general health.
- require large sums of money up front or require contracts for expensive long-term programs.
- fail to inform clients about risks associated with weight loss in general.
- don't encourage changes in habits.
- promote unproved weight-loss aids.

8

AVOIDING FRAUD AND ABUSE BY FINANCIAL PLANNERS

Anyone can call himself a financial planner and set himelf up in the business. The Consumer Federation of America calculates that there are more than 400,000 financial planners in the U.S. being used by people earning $35,000 and upwards annually. It is estimated that ten million Americans use them, rather than hassle with their own money.

While the shady operators still amount to only a small part of the industry, regulators claim that these slimy ones have committed between 150,000 to 500,000 abuses against their clients.

During 1988 and 1989 the North American Securities Administrators Association claims that 22,000 investors lost $400 million in financial-planning frauds. Even then, they say, that may represent only one-half the actual toll because reports are still coming in, claims being filed, investigations just getting underway.

Turning your money over to a financial planner without a great deal of caution and research can be committing financial suicide.

The reason people use financial planners in the

first place is because many people don't want the responsibility and work of doing the research and studying required to make sound investments!

Neither do many so-called financial planners!

Because of the bewildering number of new investment options being offered, many people feel just too confused or busy to manage their own financial affairs, and their confidence in their own savvy was shaken badly by the October 1989 market crash.

This situation has made it feast time for shady financial planners, who all seem to possess undoubting confidence in their own merit. It is this confidence that catches you like a trout.

Financial planners don't have to pass exams, as stockbrokers do. Although people who give investment advice must register with the Securities Exchange Commission, almost no one is turned down, unless there is a history of felony.

Registering means very little, anyway. It's just a few papers to fill out for filing. Enforcement is almost nonexistent. The SEC only audits planners about once every nine years and the shady ones don't stick around that long.

CERTIFIED FINANCIAL PLANNERS

The Board of Certified Financial Planners, an independent, nonprofit certifying agency, was organized in 1985 in the public interest. In order to be a Certified Financial Planner, an individual must take two years of study, and pass six national certification examinations, which take a total of two days to administer. Only approximately one-third of the 3000 who annually take the examination pass it. Some four-year institutions now offer the same registered education program offered by this agency. The passing of the exam, plus three years of experience, qualifies the individual to be a Certified Financial Planner.

The board has a strong code of ethics and an enforced disciplinary procedure. Certified Financial Planners must obtain a renewal of license annually; for this, they must continue to take courses designed to keep them up-to-date with financial information, and must have no history of wrongdoing.

There are 20,000 certified financial planners now listed with the Board of Certified Financial Planners.

Of those, 6000 have membership in the Institute of Certified Financial Planners.

Except for this certifying board and some state laws, planners are held to no testing, educational or experience standards. This looseness makes financial planning an ideal career for people with a bad past. The lack of necessary credentials means it can be used as a perfect cover.

FINANCIAL DISASTERS

This was the case for clients of the First Meridian Planning Corporation in Albany, New York. They never even suspected that the company's key promoter had a felony conviction for managing a gambling enterprise.

It wasn't until he was arrested for committing $55 million in financial planning fraud that it was discovered his only legitimate experience amounted to a high school diploma, supervising two toll booths on the Massachusetts Thruway and as a health and life insurance salesman.

The state shut down First Meridian in 1986, alleging that it raked in $55 million by getting 953 investors to pay grossly inflated prices for art, coins and Florida condos.

Some bogus financial planners entice their victims by giving free seminars, sometimes with a buffet included, and then afterwards con them into buying worthless "paper."

One questionable financial planning firm, well known in its area, used radio advertisements to scare retirees and near retirees into attending its workshops. Its ads played on the "horrors of Wall Street, the scary bond market, fluctuating interest rates" and said that if you wanted to safeguard your future you needed professional guidance such as they provided.

One couple invested their pension money — $206,000 — in a real-estate limited partnership that they were told could return up to 30 percent. Later they found that the state had shut the financial planning firm down.

A lawyer who filed a class-action suit on behalf of the defrauded investors against the firm has stated that about 2,000 people invested $50 to $60 million. He estimates that $40 million will never be recovered.

Instead of retiring, the couple have both had to find new jobs. The wife is working six days a week as a nurse and her husband, 67, a former executive, is looking for consulting work. They have been forced to put their house up for sale.

The wife is still bewildered. "I just can't believe this could happen to two people of reasonable intelligence who function well in society," she said. "Everybody had told us, 'Go to a financial planner.' "

A Richmond, Virginia financial planner was sentenced in September 1982 to 222 years in prison. He was accused by the Virginia Division of Securities and Retail Franchising of stealing $1.3 million from 40 different investors in eight different states, including $20,000 taken from his own grandmother.

One hundred investors lost $30 million to a 15-person firm that was raided July 15, 1988 by the Securities Division of the Missouri Secretary of State. The Kansas City, Missouri firm promoted nonexistent "government-backed bonds" to investors as a means of financing their children's education.

Investors nearing retirement age were the chief targets of the fraud which involved a complex web of trusts and 350 real estate limited partnerships. Investors who attended the promotional four-night seminar were promised that they could thus earn extra "tax-free" money after retirement. More than

6,000 Chicago area investors lost $45 million to these financial planners.

A Marrietta, Georgia financial planner was sentenced February 19, 1988 to five years in a federal prison for a "consumer savings certificate" swindle that cost retirees $226,000. His offer was only to Christians and made through churches.

The majority of these shady planning firms are small and hire fewer than three employees. This makes it possible for them to keep their operations fairly secret and leads to the large number of financial planning fraud and abuse cases.

Financial planners are aided and abetted by investment companies who offer them large bonuses for putting their clients' funds into their firms.

HOW TO DETECT THE HUSTLERS

A competent planner must have a firm grasp on finance and tax law. The SEC found many financial planners were new in the business and had less investment experience than their clients!

- Beware of planners who promise no-risk investments or guaranteed high returns.
- Deals involving gems, rare coins, art or condos are good signs of a bum deal.
- Cut off the transaction if the planner asks for power of attorney or discretion over your money.
- Demand solid proof of educational or experience background and check it out!

- Run, don't walk, away from planners who are not registered with state regulators or the SEC. *There has to be a good reason.*

SAFEGUARDS TO GET THE BEST PLANNERS

When hiring a financial planner, look first for a Certified Financial Planner. If you wish to find out about a specific financial planner, the Board of Cerfied Fiancial Planners will tell you whether or not he or she is certified. Call (303) 830-7543.

Another way to find a financial planner is to call the Institute of Certified Financial Planners at 800-282-PLAN and ask them for a list of certified practitioners in your area.

Remember, however, that just because an individual has met the requirements of the Board of Certified Financial Planners, that does not mean that he will make good decisions about your money. It does mean that he has the qualifications to help *you* make a decision.

Ask for references from three or more reputable clients, and talk things over with them. Get the picture straight in your mind before you work with a financial planner or let him touch your funds.

Keep in mind that losses from investment fraud in the U.S. total $40 billion a year according to the North American Securities Administration Association. Then get the basic reading on your financial planner by checking him out with your state's Securities Office.

If he passes all these tests, then you should consider hiring him. But it is still a good idea to be involved with your planning yourself. It's your life. It's your money. Who else puts your best interests first?

If you still think you need professional help in selecting investments, there are good solid ones out there. But it won't be free or cheap. The thing is to decide exactly how much help you want and just pay for that much advice. Then look past the size of the fee to see exactly how it is going to improve and affect your future.

Some financial planners charge $75 to $125 an hour. Others work on a commission basis from investments they make for you, or a commission figured at 1% or 2% a year based on increases in the value of your portfolio. Different firms have different fee arrangements depending on how much money you have to be managed and how you want it dispersed.

9

IS THAT REALLY GOLD?

More would-be investors in gold have probably been stung over the centuries than people have been stung by bees, but the scam never stops.

Whisper that you will sell them a piece of a real producing gold mine, offer to drive them out to see for themselves — and Fantasyland is no longer just at Disneyland.

Their stories could each make a book. There is something about gold fever that dwarfs all other forms of human greed. And foolishness.

People have sold their homes, cars, deserted their families, invested their entire inheritances to buy a "gold brick" that turns out to be gold-plated lead or just a pure scam.

They have stood on high windy hills in desert heats of 120° and listened in rapture while they were shown a shovel full of dirt with tiny glints of gold in it.

The promoter picks out a piece about the size of a pea.

"Now this here is pure gold!" he says. "Do you believe me now?"

The "pure gold" nugget is usually gold-plated tungsten.

Telephone marketers will tell you they are selling bank-financed precious metals. They claim they can arrange bank financing for most of the investment. Their commission devours any potential profit — if the deal was on the square.

SAD TALES

A Fort Lauderdale office manager, who received a small inheritance when her father died, plowed the entire sum into a deal that promised delayed delivery of gold at a reduced price and with monthly payments until the gold was paid in full. Then it would be delivered from the company's vault. But she never received the gold when it was paid for. There was no gold. Just a scam.

To make her plight worse, she had talked her mother into investing in the same plan. Now she is so afraid the bad news will kill her mother that she is working two jobs to make payments to her mother so she will never know that she has lost all of her money.

A New Mexico mine site promised, according to the promotor, a yield of almost $100 million in gold sales per year. A prominent San Francisco attorney was one of the 2,000 investors bilked by the swindle, losing an estimated $300,000.

An inactive Utah mine site was promoted from a jail cell by a Wyoming man serving time for already bilking 40 investors out of an average of $6,250 each.

An Oregon gold mine was promoted by a

telemarketing firm that allegedly engaged in "high pressure selling tactics and fraudulent representations." Investors have lost more than $6 million in this scam.

$10,000 GONE

Not too long ago a retired man on the East Coast thought he had finally found a chance to make it rich. He had been pitched to over the telephone by a salesman who offered him a chance to buy unprocessed, excavated soil that contained large quantities of gold.

Since he didn't consider himself a "rube," he requested that they send him documents to back up their claims. He promptly received a thick file of them.

There was a history of large gold claims that had mined millions of dollars out of that exact area in the last century and then had been abandoned because all that was left were "little nuggets" the size of peas. Solid gold peas for the picking in the dirt — but they walked away!

The papers explained the problem: in the last century they did not have the mechanized means of sifting the golden pea-sized nuggets out of the dirt. But now, if enough interested investors got together, new machinery could sift out that gold in no time at all and every investor would end up rich.

The official-looking papers provided by the promoters showed that they were the sole owners of the land and the mining rights on that property.

The papers indicated that they were keeping the investor group small so the proceeds would be big for each investor, to reward them for their faith and assistance in getting this gold to the market.

It all made sense to him and all looked official. So he promptly mailed them a check for $5,000 and within a few days received an official-looking document stating that he owned $5,000 shares in the mine.

After admiring the document for a few days and dreaming over it for a few nights, he sent another $5,000 and received a second document.

Time passed slowly. There were no more letters. No more telephone calls about the mine. So he wrote to them to find out how things were going. He received no reply.

After several written inquiries and no replies, he went to court to recover his money. But the attorney was pessimistic about his ever seeing that $10,000 again.

He is just one of thousands of people who are getting conned by "boiler room" telemarketing scams, many made from offshore the United States, selling them shares in "dirt pile" gold mines.

FOOL'S GOLD RUSH

According to the Council of Better Business Bureaus (CBBB) and the North American Securities Administrators Association, Inc. (NASAA), tens of thousands of Americans from all 50 states will be taken by these scams. NASAA believes these people will lose an estimated $250 million on dirt pile mines.

Many dirt pile gold mines seem to have appeared on the American scene after the October 1987 stock market crash, claims James C. Meyer, president of NASAA. People were suddenly so nervous about finding a safe place to put their money that they fell back on the old adage that gold is the best place to sock it.

In that mood, they were ripe plums for the picking. Since that day in October when the market looked so black, the number of gold-mine swindles have gone up from 8 to 52 and they are still rising.

This new gold rush is called the "fool's gold rush."

The NASAA says the typical dirt pile mining swindle will come on strong with a lot of excitement about the find. It will detail estimates of how much money lucky investors stand to earn — and there will be very little gold in the dirt.

Meyer claims that in many instances, investors are invited to buy 100 tons of dirt for $5,000. The promoters promise that the dirt will yield high levels of gold or other precious metals from one to three years later, processed at prices well below world market levels.

"The problem is that the gold doesn't exist, except beyond microscopic, economically unrecoverable levels," Meyer reports. "Our independent test results show that some of these supposed mine sites contain less gold than does sea water. In other words, these deals are a rip-off from the word go."

Dirt-pile mining swindles seem to share these characteristics:

- Promoters often stake out legitimate mining claims on federal land managed by the U.S. Forest Service or the Bureau of Land Management. This allows them to claim that their operations are "licensed" by the federal government.

- Mine promoters typically hire a "master broker" who sets up a telemarketing operation to push sales. In many cases, the mine, the broker and the telemarketing operation are located in different states to hinder investigations by state agencies.

- Typically, the telemarketers use "sucker lists" of people who have made questionable investments in the past and employ high-pressure sales tactics to find victims, the CBBB says.

- After the sales pitch has been made over the telephone, potential victims are sent assay documents that certify the existence of precious metals at the site, securities regulators say. But these documents are often secured from mineral testers who are either part of the scam or have worked with samples that have been doctored with extra deposits of precious metals.

There is hope that the fervor will cool if the price of gold drops steadily. It has fallen a long way since the wild rush in 1980 when it was selling for $875 an ounce.

Some commodities analysts feel that gold won't be an attractive investment until it falls below $200 an ounce. It was stated to me that "in times of rapid inflation or deflation, gold holds its value but in normal times it will lose." Economic and political conditions will influence the worth of gold again as an investment. As this book is being published, the Persian Gulf Crisis and events in the Soviet Union have driven the price up.

In the meantime, federal authorities and state securities regulators are cracking down on fraudulent dirt-pile mine scams. Better Business Bureaus are providing information to investors in an attempt to stymie telemarketing fraud.

DON'T BE A VICTIM OF "FOOL'S GOLD"

But the recipients of telemarketing sales must learn to stem the tide themselves by hanging up without listening to the pitch.

- Beware of any investment sales pitch that promises a "guaranteed" return on any investment.
- Don't be fooled by claims that something is a "secret" being shared with you!
- Remember — gold and platinum are almost never found together, so if a salesman claims

a mine contains deposits of these two precious ores, you know it is a fraud.

- Don't ever rush into any decision about investing. Talk it over with your attorney, or an investment counselor. Check the company out.
- Be skeptical of official-looking assay documents provided by the mine promoters.
- Beware if "special arrangements to pick up the money" are mentioned.
- Before investing in any "gold" deal, check out the promoter. If the promoter has violated state securities laws in the past, that information will be available to investors.

For more information, call:

The North American Securities Administration Association: (800) 942-9022. They will also supply the number for your state's securities office which provides general information about investment frauds.

Commodity Futures Trading Commission, 2033 K Street, N.W., Washington, D.C. 20581. Call (202) 254-8630 to find out if the commission has filed a complaint against the suspect futures company.

Your state securities agency or local Better Business Bureau.

10

ROMANTIC SCAMS THAT SOUR HEARTS

Love in the 90s is a lonely affair for many men and women, according to recent studies. And because it is so lonely, it can turn perfectly nice people into very embarrassed, hurt, broke, scam victims.

THE CHURCH OF LOVE

One of the saddest romance scams I uncovered took place in a tiny town in the Midwest where it was very difficult for a shy, honest working man to meet interested girls.

In that small community, teenage girls all dreamed of escaping to some big city where they would meet "Mr. Right."

They weren't interested in the seriously minded, quiet, not unattractive man who fixed cars and tractors at the local garage. He owned a small piece of land. That meant he was "planted."

Out of desperation, after receiving several pieces of mail from an organization that advertised itself as the Church of Love, he answered a postcard to become a member.

It seemed to be a dream come true. The way he describes it, it was a self-help group, a lonely hearts club, but above all it was a perfumed dream — one that held the promise of a perfect future spent in the company of beautiful, caring young women.

In exchange for a $15-$30 "love offering" to the church, he could write to anyone of the 13 Love Angels pictured in the Church of Love directory and receive one reply. He wrote to a half dozen of them but mostly to his Love Bride, a lissome brunet.

He wrote her perhaps 1,500 letters in the course of four years. He sent her pictures of his dog and his tractor and himself as a baby.

The Angels wrote back and spoke of their burning need for him. "They gave me a feeling of security, that someone really cared about me," he says.

Church of Love literature stated that all the Angels were fallen girls who had known sin in the past but they were now being "purified" back to virgins again by a young Mexican woman called Mother Maria at a type of nunnery-retreat.

They were raising money — they needed a lot of it — to build a valley paradise called Chonda-Za, a sort of heaven on earth, where the Angels of Love could devote themselves and their purified bodies for the rest of their lives to the male members of the Church of Love chosen by them.

Once an Angel had chosen a Love Man, he would receive a certificate of "exclusive reservation" of his Angel for him.

When the law investigated the Church of Love they found that Chonda-Za was pure fiction. Its

Love Angels were just models who had no idea what they were posing for. The multi-million-dollar mail-order scam was the brain-child of Donald S. Lowry, 59. He and his associate, Pamela St. Charles, were convicted of mail fraud, conspiracy and money laundering.

Tate Chambers, the assistant U.S. attorney who led the prosecution, says, "They were like medicine men in a snake-oil show. They preyed on lonely gullible men."

There were an estimated 31,000 Church of Love members across the country — men like a 56-year-old, $9-a-hour janitor at a university, who contributed almost half of his $20,000 life savings and named the Church of Love as beneficiary in his will.

"They said I could be the custodian at Chonda-Za. They promised me a servant girl and said they would take care of me the rest of my life. I was dumb, I guess." His voice was sad.

A 55-year-old truck driver from Staten Island, New York was taken for $13,000 in cash, jewelry, dresses, lingerie and other gifts. He supported the Chonda-Za building fund. "My idea was to create a community where people helped one another," he said.

Lowry gave each of his Angels a different background, personality and letter-writing style, "Like characters in a play," he said proudly. He chose the name Chonda-Za from his favorite book, James Hilton's *Lost Horizon*, and its magical setting.

The pleas for love offerings were creative and

varied: Mother Maria needed a new winter coat; Angel Audrey, who brought supplies from town, needed her car repaired. The Angels had to have garden tools to plant crops.

The biggest pitch came after the model who was known as Angel Susan had a real auto accident and was injured. Lowry wrote to Church of Love members that Angel Susan had been driving back to Mexico to visit her sick grandmother when her car was struck by a drunk driver.

He photographed Susan in the hospital, sent out the pictures and pleaded with Church of Love members to pay her medical bills. Love offerings poured in. But none of the money paid for Susan's hospital bills. She was treated as an indigent.

From 1982 through 1985 the Church of Love grossed more than $1 million a year. Lowry even opened a printing plant with 30 employees to handle the mail.

When the truth was revealed, some of the victims needed psychiatric counseling for depression. The death of a dream can bring on real mourning.

IT MAY NOT BE TRUE LOVE!

A few years ago, as a result of a speech I gave at an A.A.R.P. National Convention of Volunteers, I received a letter from a fine gentleman in Utah.

He wrote that after his wonderful wife of more than half a century passed away, he "kinda lost his head" and got trapped by a vain, selfish, self-centered, greedy gold digger who gave nothing and took all.

I can quote him saying, "I was one of the lucky widowers — it cost me $85,000 to get rid of her — but I came out of it *still alive.*"

He also explained in his letter that as a result, he had activated widowers in his city to form a weekly brunch club to give each other moral support and to steady them through the first two very vulnerable years of widowhood without doing anything foolish or letting themselves get trapped.

SOMETIMES THE LOVE BUG IS DEADLY!

In California an older woman, after a very short acquaintanceship, married a man who owned a very fine home. The marriage was just about as short as the acquaintanceship had been.

As soon as he moved into her house, they put his house up for sale and it sold immediately. Almost as soon as the escrow was closed, the bride declared the groom "incapable of handling his own affairs," got a durable power of attorney over all of his personal business, divorced him and put him in a nursing home. After a couple of months he was declared penniless and Medicare and Medicaid had to pay his bills.

She used the money that was now hers to take a prolonged cruise to Hawaii, Tahiti, Samoa, New Zealand, Australia, Hong Kong, Singapore and finally Japan.

Since he had no family, neither did he have visitors or anyone to speak up for him. She is quite smug about her "business deal."

IT HAPPENS TO WOMEN, TOO

One of the jobs I frequently handled as a private investigator was to take a woman to a ranch that our agency maintained after a lover had stolen her money and her car and abused her on a Friday night. It was impossible to get a restraining order or any help from the courts until the courts opened on Monday morning, so our agency cared for such clients for the weekend.

These women were usually attractive, successful business women in their late 40s or early 50s.

The man was often a playboy of their own age, the charming type that was hired as a host on cruise ships to entertain single women. A Las Vegas high roller, he played excellent golf, tennis, bridge and was a wonderful dancer. He always had a line as smooth as whipped cream.

Everything about him was too good to be true, but loneliness and vanity helped these women believe his phony line.

One of the most unique romantic twists regarding men as romantic scammers is that of the bigamist who married seven "wives"and cleaned them all out. The "wives," from various parts of the country, have now formed their own posse club and they are united in their effort to catch him!

CLASSIFIED AD MATCH MAKING

An increasing number of newspapers and

magazines directed toward mature readers are now running match-making classified ads under various departmental names.

The people who advertise are not all dullards or undesirables. A woman minister admitted in a magazine article that she is running an ad. Why? Because it is difficult for a woman minister to date or meet a potential mate. A male minister has a pool of widows to choose from. A male member of her congregation would feel intimidated.

But — warning!

Since there is no screening of the people who place these ads, it must be remembered that danger lurks in meeting strangers.

It is recommended that the best way to meet on a first date is over coffee in a busy coffee shop. It is easy to leave and no harm can be done.

If you place an ad yourself, make sure the return address is a blind post office box; sometimes the newspaper will provide such blind boxes. Do not list your home address or telephone number, and do not share it until you are convinced that the person you are meeting for the first time is trustworthy.

Since the happiest and most successful marriages still are reported to be those among people who went to school together at some time in their lives, or attended the same church, or were introduced by friends, or met through a hobby or their business, maybe men and women are all looking too far from home for romance.

11

STAGED AUTOMOBILE ACCIDENTS SPIRAL YOUR INSURANCE

There are nearly 3,600 staged auto accidents a year in California alone, according to Ronald E. Warthen, Chief Investigator, Fraud Bureau, State of California Department of Insurance. The gross incomes for suspect attorneys who are involved range from $500,000 to $1 million annually. One Northern California medical clinic, involved in such fraud, had a gross income of $750,000 in 1987, and paid over $300,000 for attorney referrals.

If you don't live in California, your state will have similar figures, depending on population of cities and their affluence.

Insurance frauds of all kinds are a big threat to us and our economy. They deplete our savings, cut into our earnings, cheat us on health care, deprive us of security.

In big cities at the present time, but most especially in Southern California where automobile congestion is the greatest (it is catching up in Florida and other states), faked auto accidents are proliferating. These accidents are as well rehearsed as plays on the stage, which is why they are called *staged* auto accidents.

These are accidents where everyone pays except the scam artists. Every person who is paying automobile insurance pays a higher premium so that the leeches, who are chiefly crooked lawyers and doctors, can line their pockets. The victim, an innocent person just driving his car, unaware that he is being set up for an accident, will be hurt financially, and sometimes psychologically and physically.

In the beginning are the lawyers. They hire a criminal to deliberately cause automobile accidents. He is given "up-front" money, often as much as $10,000, to stage a certain number of these phoney crashes.

In these accidents, *ghost* people sue for a great number of personal injuries that do not occur. They are called ghosts because they are usually unsuspecting people picked up as props by the scam driver. They never again have anything to do with the claim. They may never even be aware that their name is being used for a claim.

The insurance money never goes to those claiming they were injured, or to the scam driver. It is divided between the attorney and his henchman doctor.

The chief victim is the insurance company, followed by all the people holding the policies with that company. But the one who suffers the most is the baffled person who can't figure out how he had the accident or how anyone got hurt so badly.

And, of course, he gets a bad mark on his driving records, which shoots up his insurance premium.

IT HAPPENED TO GRACE

One such accident happened to a friend of mine. Grace collects aluminum cans at her church. The men of the church have built a smasher for her, and they help her load the flattened cans into her car.

Once a week she drives to a recycling plant and gets the money from the cans, which has been used to make life easier for the elderly people of the congregation. She has been doing this for over a year.

One quiet day, just as she emerged from the recycling plant, she had a very minor fender-bender with another woman exiting the same premises. Both felt that they were at fault. They were very happy to find that they had so little damage, and because they were both insured with the same company, neither would have to pay deductible.

They thought it was all settled. A week later they were both informed that the passenger in Grace's car had filed for personal soft tissue injuries.

With the notification in her hands, Grace grabbed her telephone. "What passenger? There was no one in the car but me!"

"She claims she was in your back seat, helping you, and she was knocked to the floor."

Grace still had the telephone number of the woman who collided with her.

"Did you see a passenger in the back seat of my car?"

"No. And I just got a letter, too. She's filed a claim against me, also. When I called the insurance office they said she told them I couldn't see her because she fell off the seat onto the floor."

"There was no room for a passenger in my back seat. It was full of a month's collection of smashed cans!"

Grace drove to the recycling plant. John, who always helped her, was on duty that day.

"Did you see a passenger in my car the last time I was here?"

"I was so busy, I didn't notice. But I remember you had more cans than usual." John looked at her small car. "That Colt wouldn't have had room for a passenger with all those cans, would it?"

"You better believe it didn't!"

Grace called the insurance representative again. "I'm sorry, but the woman has described you, your car, the upholstery in your car, your conversation with the recycler, your home, your church, your clothes."

"What the heck is her name?" Grace asked.

When she heard the name, she shook her head. "Never heard of her!"

Hartford then fed the supposed injured victim's name into their computer system and discovered that during the past year the woman had filed six claims for injuries suffered while she was a back seat passenger. In every case the driver did not know the woman. State insurance fraud investigators arrested the so-called passenger.

She had picked her victims by hanging around the recycling plant and listening, then following her intended victims home. She'd spend about one month observing all their personal habits, especially the hours and days that they regularly drove places. She had an accomplice who worked on people she befriended at churches.

After studying the victim's habits, the accomplice hid near the known site at the time the victim usually appeared. He had a small dog in his arms. At the exact moment when Grace was passing near the other woman's car at the narrow entrance that led out of the recycling plant, he dropped the dog.

Both women were distracted by the dog just long enough to crash into each other. The other driver was unlucky enough to be involved. But Grace was the intended victim.

THE TWO-CAR STAGED ACCIDENT

A favorite scam makes an innocent victim the one who supposedly caused the accident. This is accomplished by using two cars. The one ahead of the chosen victim will usually be a beat-up, large old-model car with three or four men in it.

The car will ride along in front of the victim-driver for quite awhile until the victim-driver gets used to having that car in front of him.

Another car will ride along beside the victim-driver and every time the driver tries to pass the lumbering car in front, the car on the side will speed up.

Then one of two things will happen. The car on the side will do something to attract the attention of the victim so he will look away from the car in front for just a second — and bam! — hit the other car which for no apparent reason has stopped dead.

Or the car on the side will suddenly speed up, dive in front of the lumbering car, forcing it to slam on its brakes and the victim will slam into that car.

In either case, the victim is responsible for the accident. The passengers in the lumbering car will all complain of severe pain. The victim will be puzzled about how they could be hurt that badly.

Their scam doctors and lawyers will take over from there and sue the victim's insurance for all it can get. Frequently the "injured passengers" will receive no treatment whatever. They will just fill out forms with their signature repeated down the sheet. The scam doctor will fill in the dates when he claims he saw them and treated them.

THE DRIVEWAY ACCIDENT AND MORE

Another trick occurs when you are trying to back out of your driveway. After being certain there are no witnesses watching, the scam artists motion you to go ahead and then they quickly drive behind you and deny that they waved you out of the driveway.

Scam auto accident players usually pick a good neighborhood where people drive good cars and therefore are sure to be covered by substantial automobile insurance.

The "players" look for older people, especially elderly

couples or women driving newer model cars. Affluent women are considered to be more responsible about keeping their insurance up to date.

They pick congested areas where people are preoccupied, hurried. They keep an eye open for a prospective victim who is doing something slightly illegal so the law will be on their side. They watch for someone making an illegal left turn, making a rolling instead of a dead stop at a red light, someone making a lane change by cutting into a line in order to make a left or right turn, or crossing a double yellow line to reach an address.

They always endeavor to run into the victim so that their own side quarter of the car is smashed. That is the easiest way to blame the other driver and not get seriously hurt.

Some of these scammers stage as many as four or five accidents a day. A team of unscrupulous doctors and lawyers can have two or three drivers working for them, staging as many as ten accidents a day — every day.

HOW CAN YOU AVOID A STAGED ACCIDENT?

The best insurance against getting caught in a staged auto accident is to drive carefully and within the law, and to always be aware of all the cars around you. What are they doing?

Never tailgate. If you get in an emergency and are tailgating, you have no room to escape. If a car seems to be hanging around you too long, turn off, slow down, find a way of losing it.

Staged automobile accidents are never performed on busy freeways because the actors don't want to risk *really* getting hurt. It is busy boulevards that have two or three lanes going each direction that they choose most often.

Older women especially are thrown off balance by a friendly person who seems warmly interested in their life. They ignore the fact that they are being questioned, almost cross-examined, during the course of the conversation which seems focused on them.

When new acquaintances ask too many personal questions, steer away from them. They might be just nosey gossips. Then again, they may be setting you up for something. Keep your personal life confined to close friends and relatives.

If you do get into an auto accident, get as much information about the car that you hit as possible. Get the identification of all the passengers in that car. Look for independent witnesses. Get their names, addresses and telephone numbers.

Never give any information other than the law requires. Remember that 25% of all insurance premiums go for fraud investigations and prosecutions. Don't help the scam artists!

12

JOB COUNSELORS WHO SCALP

It's sad enough to find yourself entering the prime of your life, having had a successful career for quite a few years, unemployed before you were ready or willing to retire. Then you may find that in your desperate search to regain a footing, you have been taken by a scam artist who charged you dearly for empty promises.

It happens because frequently people like you, especially those who held professional jobs, were managers or other executives, will seek out a professional job counseling service to help them get back into the work force.

And, because of this, fraudulent employment agencies (scam firms) are leaving a growing trail of fleeced victims. Such firms are flourishing all across the country, despite legal attempts to stop them.

They use ads tucked away in the classifieds. They entice victims by claiming they can open the "hidden job market." There is no such thing as a hidden job market.

They brag that they have secret connections with employers and computerized data bases to match the client with openings anywhere in the country.

The truth is, authorities have found, that many of the disreputable firms offer nothing more than badly written resumes and outdated lists of corporate contacts which they have usually clipped from newspaper ads or have found easily in directories of corporations available in public libraries.

For all this sham, some of these firms charge as much as $6,000 *in advance*. They go after white-collar executives. Other victims are blue-collar workers dreaming of working overseas.

The problem has grown so vast that in every one of the 50 states, law enforcement agencies have set up offices to answer questions about advance-fee employment services.

The victims are usually people who are desperately in need of a job and therefore fall for it hook, line and sinker. In the present job situation which the 90s face, there will be even more people to be fleeced. Some people from middle or upper management jobs, finding themselves helpless without work, will squander their entire separation pay. It has led to some suicides.

In Ft. Lauderdale, Florida police have revealed that one firm, Automated International Placements, through its pitches swayed more than 2,000 people to pay them more than $750,000 for jobs that never even existed.

In 1989 the New York attorney general's office investigated Hinkler, Reid and Stevenson, a firm in Albany, New York. They found that there were no hidden jobs, no personal contact was made with companies, and resumes and cover letters were usually never mailed, just put in piles to collect dust in the office. They were charged with conning $200,000 from 75 clients.

But chasing down these scam agencies isn't easy. Law enforcement agencies find that they use fake names more often than snakes shed their skins. Often they close up after only a couple of months, disappear, open under a different name in a distant state.

They get around state bans on employment agencies charging payment in advance by not calling themselves employment agencies. They are *career counseling* or *career consulting* businesses.

In most states executive search associations, job counselors, career marketing firms — whatever title they choose for themselves, *need no credentials* except those that they give themselves.

Sometimes they need a license. In some states they do not. There is no test to pass. No qualifications to meet. They can just place Yellow Pages, newspaper and magazine ads, rent an office, have their name painted on the door, rent some furniture and hire a temporary secretary-receptionist.

The qualities they all seem to have in common are confidence in themselves, a charming manner, nice clothes, and a way of wangling themselves into your confidence — more *confidence* men.

Most of them will demand a fee of $3,000 upwards, often in advance, when they sign you up. It will be for testing you, faxing your availability about the country, rewriting your resume. They may add a dozen other services that they propose to perform.

Actually the shoe is on the wrong foot. You should start out by interviewing them and checking on them before you pay any fee! You're going to be giving them a lot of confidential information that can make you very vulnerable.

About the only thing they will willingly tell you about themselves is that they "have a high rate of placement" in "high-paying jobs," and can save you energy, heartbreak and wasted time in your search. This is because, "through personal contacts with top executives at Fortune 500 (or whatever) corporations, they have secret knowledge of jobs that need to be filled."

They often claim to have placed around 95% of all their clients "in better positions than they held before they made their change."

Remember, there is no limit on what they may charge you for their counseling. Unless your advance fee was a hefty one, every time you report back to them for a follow-up, it is going to cost you more money.

When a client begins to question the promises of the sales representatives and perhaps do a little investigation into the firm, or causes it to come under the scrutiny of a government investigation or a media exposé, or files a lawsuit charging misrepresentation and false promises, these career marketing services have a way of suddenly going bankrupt and their owners disappearing.

FINDING THE GOOD GUYS

Because there are many sound career management firms with good reputations, it is therefore necessary for you to know how to go about finding the good guys.

The Federal Trade Commission and other regulators offer the following advice:

Before you even appear for your first interview with a career planning firm, do a little research on your own. Check with local consumer protection agencies and the state attorney general's office to see if they have had any complaints about the company and about laws regulating the industry.

If they come up clean, then proceed to your interview. Be sure to read the *written* contract and do not put too much weight on what the sales representative promises you. If he won't put his glorious promises in writing in the contract, keep your wallet and check book in your pocket. He isn't to be trusted.

Advertisements have a way of being unclear. From the moment you make contact, make it a point to find out exactly what the company is offering, exactly what they are promising, exactly how much their services cost and who pays for them.

If all the money is to come out of your pocket,

then find out the terms and if you are required to pay even if they fail to find you a position.

Keep reminding yourself during the salesman's smooth pitch, that a company can only promise to help you find a job, it cannot guarantee it. If they say they can guarantee it, excuse yourself. Your sick mother has been waiting in the car too long.

Remember, the better the job you held before you ran into the wolves' den, the more guilt and embarrassment you will feel for being such a fool!

Regular employment agencies advertise specific openings in companies. Often the fee the agency charges for finding you for the job is paid by the hiring company, but sometimes part of the fee is billed to you. It always happens after you have the job.

Executive search firms often are hired by a business to find the right person for a very specific job. In that case, the person who is hired never pays the fee.

A new career resources center may be the best place for you. They provide you with the skills, training and moral support to get out there and present yourself in a win-win attitude. They review and sometimes rewrite your resume. But they don't promise you a job. They advise you about how to find the job, and the footwork is up to you. They believe that no one ever works as hard for you as you do for yourself, so they give you the skills and the moral support. Their fees run around $55.

Career counseling services provide general advice and assistance with job-hunting techniques and resume advice, but they have no specific job in mind. Their fees range from $1,000 to $4,000, which must often be paid in advance and there is no waiving of the fee or returning even a portion of it if you fail to find a job.

Before you get caught in what might turn out to be one of these hideous webs, be sure and seek out all the *free* opportunities that are available to you!

- State job-service offices post vacancies and provide some counseling.
- County human resources offices can provide placement help and referrals.
- University and college career services often have job centers.
- So do local public libraries.

13

SWINDLES THAT CAPTURE YOU BY TELEPHONE

Telephone scams wring big money out of the millions of U.S. investors who have become accustomed to conducting stock and bond trades over the telephone with their brokers.

Because it is normal for legitimate brokers to solicit new business by telephone, crooks get away with cold calls by passing themselves off as legitimate Wall Street brokers recommended by one of your friends.

By using this method, they have talked elderly investors into investing large sums, even borrowing heavily against their home equity, to buy into schemes which they claim are "the surest on the market to be going places."

Lower international long-distance rates enable phone scammers to move to locations such as Costa Rica or the Bahamas — you can't tell where the call is originating — and there they are harder to prosecute.

As a result, John Baldwin, president of the North American Securities Administrators Association, says, "We are facing a national epidemic of truly staggering proportions."

WHO WOULD GIVE MONEY TO A STRANGER?

One wonders: who on earth would send thousands of dollars to a complete stranger for nothing more than verbal assurances of a quick profit?

Who? Well, bankers, executives, lawyers, housewives, financial advisers, celebrities, retirees, physicians, farmers, educators and countless others with starry-eyed visions of wealth. The thing that they most share in common is that they become poorer as a result.

- A young Illinois high school teacher sent an inherited $40,000 to a hard-sell commodities broker in Florida. Soon afterward the outfit was closed down by federal agents.

- In Kansas City a couple lost several thousand dollars they had saved to pay college tuition for their children.

- A Texas woman was talked out of $11,000 by a long distance pitchman. She complained to the Federal Trade Commission, which recovered the money. Three months later she lost it to another con artist.

- To provide an income for the care of his brain-damaged child, a man sold his home and invested over $30,000 of the proceeds in unregistered securities. Soon afterward he discovered he had been taken. He was so upset that he killed himself.

- Many of the victims are retired people on fixed incomes. They either are too lonely or too polite to hang up on the pitches. One 84-year old woman in Georgia lost $20,000 to a "nice young man" who said he was a "native Nebraska boy brought up with high morals" who talked her into investing in a movie production to help him make his talents known.

- Unable to work any longer because of ill health, a man invested his life savings of $45,000 in privately placed securities. He lost it all.

- A woman in her 80s put $37,500 into what was described as a recreational resort and an oil and gas venture. The promoter stole every cent.

- A widow with five children was talked into investing in a tax-shelter scheme which lost all of her money. She didn't even need a tax-shelter as she had no taxable income!

- From March 1979 through May 1980, Wilbert A.Wilson, 40, of New York City, a former electrician, rented an office, installed a battery of telephones, hired salespeople and sold participation units in commodity pools. (Commodity futures are contracts that guarantee future delivery at current prices of farm products, precious metals and various other commodities. If prices go up in the meantime, the contracts can be sold at a profit.)

He collected $3,400,00 which he pocketed after sharing a small amount with his sales force. When arrested he was accused of operating a *ponzi* scheme, in which early investors are paid "profits" with money sent in by later ones and then are talked into getting in deeper and deeper.

- The biggest ponzi scheme to date sold $130 million in oil and gas drilling participation units to well known Hollywood stars, at least one senator and the chairman of one of the nation's largest banks.

The con artists didn't have to work very hard to scam some of these people.

Apparently the victims did not know that federal law requires pool operators (a pool is funds from more than one investor combined with others in a so-called investment) to furnish prospective investors with performance data.

This data must cover the three preceding years (or the entire period of the pool's operation if less than three years), plus information about the company and its principals, methods of trading, expenses, and risks.

MORE TELEPHONE "HOOKS"

Some of the abuse comes by way of 900 numbers which seem to be bad news in all cases. Never let your fingers walk on those numbers! If you do, you will hear recorded messages costing $5 to $50, usually to dispense worthless or generic information on subjects including credit repair and social security benefits, all of which you can get for free elsewhere.

MORTGAGE ACCELERATION SCHEMES

Another deal offered by telemarketing is the hawking of bimonthly mortgages, and these are usually a very bad idea. You'll pay higher fees, give someone else interest-free use of the extra money you pay each month until the end of the year, and risk trouble if the third party fails to make payments.

This advice comes from the Alliance Against Fraud in Telemarketing, which lists mortgage acceleration schemes among the top ten phone scams it expects will plague you in the 90s.

SWINDLER TESTIMONY

In July 1990, two convicted swindlers who had run very successful but fraudulent telephone marketing "boiler rooms" explained to Congress how their salesmen were able to bilk over $75 million dollars out of innocent "mooches" by selling them phoney rare coin and oil-lease schemes.

And this was just one boiler room. The total tab for these scams is estimated to be in the billions of dollars.

The testimony of the telephone swindlers, using aliases, wearing black hoods, sitting behind screens and speaking through a voice modulator was being used in Congress for study to find ways to change federal laws so they would help enforcement officials crack down on these telephone scams.

WHAT ARE THEY SELLING?

These fraudulent salesmen may offer you an investment based on the scarcity of a foreign metal after news of a trade embargo, or they might offer you an investment in a new, widely publicized high-tech product.

But they pitch many other things, too. Their most popular snares included rare coins, gemstones, oil and gas leases, interests in oil wells, applications for cellular telephone licenses, the sale of precious metals such as gold and silver, or strategic metals such as chromium used in defense or high-tech industries.

Another telemarketing scam is foreign banking schemes. You're told that foreign banking laws allow overseas banks to offer extremely high rates of return. But your investments frequently disappear as soon as they are collected.

Telephone scammers like to pitch investments that the average person knows very little about. But they can also be vacations, bargains on fake expensive furs, perfumes and gems.

They operate out of boiler room settings filled with desks, telephones, and salesmen who spend their days calling hundreds of prospects all over the country.

YOU'RE NEXT

If you own a telephone, you stand a good chance of receiving a telephone pitch. Having an unlisted telephone number is no protection as numbers are dialed by computer, number following number until someone answers.

You may be called if you responded to an ad or filled out a card asking for more information about an investment, or you might be called "cold."

Their voices are always warm and friendly. But watch out for key sentences such as, "You must act now. We're closing this deal tonight." "There will be huge tax write-offs. . ." or "There's already a long list of people waiting to get a piece of this." When you hear those hackneyed phrases, you know you have a scam on the phone.

Since your caller is selling on commission and anxious to keep moving right along, you might do some unknown person a good favor if you just say to him, "Excuse me a moment, there is someone at the door. . ." and let him hold the phone until he finally gets the point that you have reversed roles and tricked him.

Don't let curiosity, loneliness or just being bored tempt you to talk to such scammers. If you saw a rattlesnake on your doorstep, would you invite it in? Listening to a telephone boiler room hustler is the same thing. They are both out to kill.

For a free booklet entitled *Swindlers Are Calling,* write to:

Alliance Against Fraud in Telemarketing
c/o National Consumers League
815 15th Street NW, Suite 928
Washington, DC 20005

CHARITY WARNING

Before giving any money to a charity that you're not familiar with, send $1.00 and a self-addressed stamped envelope for the booklet *Give . . . But Give Wisely* to:

Philanthropic Advisory Service
4200 Wilson Blvd.
Arlington, VA 22203

Or write for *Wise Giving Guide* to:

National Charities Information Bureau
19 Union Square W
Sixth Floor
New York, NY 10003-3395

In all cases, refuse to make a commitment to over-the-phone solicitations for gifts and charities: they may turn out to be nonexistent. Ask them to send you more information, and call your local Better Business Bureau to see if the organization meets the Better Business Bureau's standards.

Also be wary of people raising money with a high-pressure appeal for heart-rending causes. Like disasters. Demand identification and further information from organizations before you give. Ask questions — find out where your dollar is going. Always pay by check.

14

NEW CAR AND MOTOR HOME RIP-OFFS

"Whenever I buy a new car," a savvy businessman once told me, "after I get home I find that no matter how careful I have been about watching and listening to the salesman, I count my fingers and sure enough, one of them is missing! I just hate buying cars. I wish there was some other method of getting a new car than being attacked by commission-hungry sharks."

I agree! Daring to step into a new car showroom seems exactly the same as entering a den of rattlesnakes.

This is one time in your life when seeking out the least experienced salesperson on the floor might be an advantage.

But it won't be for long, because the manager will quickly pull you into his office and then the double talk and giggle figures will be thrown at you, and you will begin to feel light-headed.

The only way to approach the buying of a new car is to accept the fact that you are going to be approached as a sucker, so do a month's homework before you step inside the door.

Know exactly what you are looking for. What its

wholesale price is. What features you want. How much you are willing to pay. If the pressure and climate get too hot, depart.

Even if you think you have it all figured out, watch those figures the finance manager is tossing around. One of the sleekest tricks may occur after you have agreed on the price and start to pay cash for the car (you decided that almost a year ago and have been setting the cash aside for this big day): the salesman doesn't happily accept your check.

Instead he backs away from it like it's an uzi gun and steers you to the "finance man." Why? You aren't trying to finance anything. But the finance man then brings out the giggle figures and runs through them very rapidly. He may use a computer or a VCR, but what he is trying to prove to you is that it is cheaper for you, in the long run, to finance the car, and invest your money in something else.

Anyone knows that paying cash for anything is cheaper than paying off a loan on it. Those interest rates eat up your money. But the finance man produces a computer print-out that twists your mind through a maze to prove that you have been taught all wrong.

Why is he doing this to you? *Because the car dealership makes more money from the loan it makes to you than it does from selling the car!* Just add up the interest on such a loan!

The computer program that you are shown, to convince you, is rigged so that it fails to show the income taxes you will have to pay on the money you leave in the bank or money market account while you pay off the loan. That way it makes it look like you are coming out ahead.

To figure it correctly, you must subtract the interest paid on the loan, and the income taxes, from the amount of interest earned by the sum if left in a savings or money market account. Then add in the trade-in price of your car in, say, five years.

You don't have to have an electric head to see that the computer printout is lying to you and that you will come out with a nice little sum of savings by paying cash.

If you press them to the wall, car dealers will admit this computer show is in error but they shrug it off as "advertising. No one expects advertising to be 100% true."

PREPAYMENT REFUND

Another trick used by car dealers is known as the *prepayment refund.* If you are financing your car, the dealer will choose one of two options. These options are "the rule of 78" or "the sum of periodic time balance method." There are no other options offered on the contracts.

This is new car dealer gibberish. It promises you will not have to pay a prepayment penalty for paying off your car loan early. But you will not save on interest which you pay in full just as if you didn't prepay.

It makes no difference which way you go, because

whether you do or do not prepay your loan, either way you will end up paying more interest than you would earn in a bank account of the same interest rate paying compound interest. This is a scam!

However, these methods are in accordance with the Department of Consumer Affairs Federal Reserve Bank Pamphlet — but the Internal Revenue Service does not allow these methods when calculating interest deductions for tax purposes!

Car buyers have won one inning: The National Highway Traffic Safety Administration's Auto Safety Hotline. Consumers can now call a hot line, (800) 424-9393, to find out if a car model is known to have a safety defect without having to take the word of any fast-talking salesman.

But you still have to watch some of the other charges on your car purchase. Some dealers overcharge on the state auto registration, insurance fees and sales tax.

In one of the worst federally prosecuted cases against a car dealership, poor farm workers, pensioners with no savings and barely able to get by on their small income, and young soldiers from a nearby Army base were enticed to come in and look at new models of cars that were available for very low monthly payments of $180 or so.

Out of curiosity they walked into the lion's den. When they left, even though they had no intention of buying a car, many were driving a new late-model car. They believed that their monthly payments were to be very low and within their reach.

However, they discovered that their true payments were upwards of $400 per month. The purchasers of these cars found that they could not return them. And there was no way that they could make $400-a-month car payments.

In order for this to happen, employees of the dealership filed false loan applications to make customers appear to be better candidates for credit. They reported rebates as down payments, falsified trade-in deals, allowed customers to make down payments in installments and listed nonexistent "add-on" luxuries such as air conditioning, power windows, stereo systems to inflate the price of the cars.

The bank wound up financing cars at higher than their value. The prices of the cars were inflated so much that in many cases they were doubled.

When the case was investigated by the F.B.I., it was found that a half-dozen top sales and finance officials from the dealerships had submitted false customer credit applications, loan documents and sales contracts to the Bank of America.

In one case, the sales contract submitted was $14,000 for a car with a wholesale value of $6,000. (Bank loans only finance the wholesale price of a car. The down payment and trade-in make up the difference between the bank loan and the retail price.) The sales contract said the purchaser's new car was a loaded two-door model with sport wheels. According to testimony produced in court, it actually was a stripped station wagon that didn't even have a radio.

The bank loan application on this same car stated that the purchaser had traded in a 1973 Chevrolet Malibu for $1,000. The purchaser testified he had never owned one. He was promised a $3,000 rebate — but of course the check never came.

It took the jury of six men and six women less than two hours of deliberation to find the former finance manager guilty of two counts of falsifying customer credit applications. Five other defendants including the former president and part-owner pleaded guilty.

Consumer Reports, a nonprofit national organization, provides car buyers with a list of dealers' costs for automobiles and options. The list costs $10 for one car model, $18 for two, $25 for three and $8 for each additional. It is available from:

> Consumer Reports
> P.O. Box 570
> Lathrup Village, MI 48076

SERVICE CONTRACTS?

On top of all the decisions and headaches you have already gone through to buy the car, you must now decide whether to purchase a service contract. Should you or shouldn't you fork over another $500 or so?

Consumer advocates say service contracts are a bad deal. They point out the large profit margins to the dealer who sells the contract to you.

Many of these contracts restrict coverage severely but seldom put it in easily read language. Don't read the long list of things covered — read the exclusions. This is where you get unpleasant surprises.

Exclusions commonly refuse to cover damage caused by an uncovered part. A gasket is never a covered part, but it can damage the engine if it fails. The engine will then be uncovered!

Plans will not cover damage if proper maintenance requirements are not followed. An engine that overheats on a long, hot trip on a congested mountain highway due to low coolant may produce a large repair bill, but no coverage.

Before you buy, find out:

- Who's behind it? The best are backed by the manufacturer.
- What are your duties? Many contracts exclude coverage unless maintenance follows their schedule in the maintenance manual and you must have proof if you do it elsewhere.
- Does it have a deductible?
- Must the repairs be done only at authorized dealers?
- What does the service contract give you that the warranty doesn't?
- Who will arbitrate if your claim is denied and you disagree?

MOBILE HOME AND CAMPER RIP-OFFS

Camino Camper, Inc., the self-proclaimed leader in recreational vehicles in Northern California, with six outlets in San Jose, Hayward, Arizona and Nevada, has been accused by the Department of Motor Vehicles and the district attorney of not forwarding to the bank lenders, the payments made to them by customers on loans for their recreational vehicles.

At the time of this writing lenders have filed separate law suits seeking the payment of loans and damages totaling more than $5.4 million and the repossession of scores of vehicles. Some of the vehicles had cost as much as a home.

The investigation is uncovering other companies in this business that have also failed to transfer the buyers' payments for license fees and insurance. And some dealerships have failed to pay off a buyer's original loan when a used vehicle is traded in, leaving the original buyer liable for the loan and the second-hand buyer without title to the vehicle.

Other abuses found in recreational vehicle sales include "switch and bait"(engaging in misleading advertising), modifying contract terms after contracts were signed, falsifying or omitting financial information on credit applications, and failing to cancel contracts and return down payments or trade-ins, as required by law, when consumers are unable to obtain financing.

15

ROBBERS IN THE AUTO REPAIR BUSINESS

VAGABOND THIEVES, PIRATES AND HIGHWAY ROBBERS

Vagabond thieves frequently do auto body repair work to earn extra money. They drive around town looking for dented automobiles and, after locating one and its owner, they inform the owner that they can make the repairs cheaply. After the work is done the thieves may say the job was complicated and charge an exorbitant fee.

There are also pirates out there on the highways and byways. These pirates drive tow trucks looking for unwary drivers. If you break down and call for your auto club to come help you, be certain that the tow truck that arrives first is the one authorized by your auto club. If a pirate arrives first, and you are not aware of, you may be charged many times the towing fee — which will not be covered by your auto club.

Often they will tow you to a garage where they get a commission for the number of cars they bring in for repair. *Always look on the side of the tow truck for the insignia of your auto club!* Otherwise don't open your doors or windows. Just wait for your own truck, a state trooper or the highway patrol.

There are also highway robbers out there, and they come in all sizes and shapes. Sometimes they even look like college students studying to be doctors and lawyers — and that is exactly what they are. They're earning extra money on vacations.

A number of years back, I picked up a tip about these highway men along the roads that run through the American desert regions, so I went out to see for myself.

It was Christmas season and the freeway was packed with people going and coming from family reunions, skiing resorts, Las Vegas.

Before I started on my journey, my editor informed me, "When I travel through the wide open spaces, I never leave my car in front of the pumps while I use the washrooms or go next door to a restaurant. I always move it. I've heard too many stories about cars being damaged by the station attendants."

When I did find the culprits, they were clean-cut, smartly dressed college types operating in a large glossy major oil station in New Mexico.

During almost 5,000 miles of travel, through sub-freezing temperatures, high winds in the West, hail in Missouri, sleet in Indianapolis, I had found attendants at all the major oil company stations to be honest, courteous and efficient. I had also noted how many of them advertised **Mechanic on Duty 24 Hours**. For a traveler that was very important.

In New Mexico, a large banner proclaiming **Free Safety Check** could be seen for a mile before I reached the gas cut-off from the freeway.

Even before I stopped, I noted that almost every one of their repair bays was filled while travelers stood by, shivering in the intense chill. In fact, hearty, jaunty, clean-cut college types were waving cars into the bays like it was a day at the races. One of them bounced up to serve me when I stopped.

I had been warned what to be on the lookout for and wasn't surprised when I noticed he was wearing an unusually large ring with a mounting that came to a sharp point at his knuckles. I'd been told this was used to slash hoses and tires, so I slid down in the front seat to watch very closely through the bottom of the hood after he raised it.

"You've got to get a new battery," he informed me immediately. "It's overheating and burning up your voltage regulator. It's causing your alternator to overwork and it will burn up in a few more miles if you don't replace the battery and regulator."

"I had the car serviced the day before yesterday and everything checked out okay. Besides, there's no light on the dashboard."

"Ma'am, if the light was on," he explained, "then it would already be too late." He said the battery would cost $90, the regulator $38.95, plus labor. But it could save me $300 or more than the cost if the alternator burned up.

While he was talking, I was watching a van with a

New Jersey license plate pull in beside me. Within minutes two attendants were waving it into the repair bay. I saw three very upset old people, a man and two women, get out of the van, and then it was shot up on the hoist.

When I told him I'd like to get another diagnosis (I could see a half dozen stations at this oasis) he took my credit card to write up my purchase. But then I noticed him doing something odd. He called someone on the phone and I could tell from the way he was looking at me and my car that he was giving them a description of me, and arguing with them.

I surmised that he was advising someone, possibly of the same oil company, to give the same diagnosis and split the commission. So I sought out an independent station, a truck stop, reasoning they were less apt to cheat truckers.

I apologized to the mechanic for bringing him out into the stinging cold when I didn't need gas (by then it was obvious that a blizzard was imminent) but I asked him to check out my battery. He did and said everything was fine. I explained the other diagnosis and asked if it were possible.

His eyes grew dark with anger. He pointed back down the road.

"It was that station, wasn't it?" Then he told me the alternator would have to be running wild, overworking the voltage regulator, to burn up the battery. The reverse, as the other station claimed, absolutely could not occur.

THE AUTO PARTS STORE

My next adventure with the auto repair business happened when my son was fixing his car and asked me to drive down to the auto parts store to get him a part he needed. He wrote down the description and handed me a $20 bill.

First, I discovered it is almost impossible for a woman alone to get waited on at this auto parts store. After the man had located the part, he studied the price in the thick catalog and quoted more than $20.

Instead of buying it, I went back home and asked my son about that price. He started to clean his hands immediately.

"Come along, Mom, I'll show you how it works. In that catalog they have three different prices. One for people in the repair business. One for men customers. And one for women."

At that time my son was night manager of a gas station that did only small repairs. I changed my blouse to a T-shirt before we went back to the store.

This time we were waited on almost immediately. The price quoted was $11! Then my son showed his paycheck stub and the price dropped to $7.50.

AUTO SCAMS ARE AS COMMON AS FLEAS

In the years since then I have had many women wail to me, "I'll never take my car in for repairs unless I have a man with me!" They have reported all kinds of wild gouging when they went alone.

Recently a television program showed three investigators, with a car that was in 100% perfect shape, checking out the auto repair industry. At different times on the same day, they each took it to repair shops. Two of the drivers were women. They received very high quotes for repairs. The man received a small quote. They then took the car to a diagnostic center. The car came out clean. It needed no work of any kind.

A woman who worked for a short time in the same room with me on one of the newspapers, told me, "Never take your car to ------. My husband worked there and he quit because he got sick of being forced to cheat."

A neighbor advised me, "Never take your car for repairs to a new car dealership. You have to pay for all their overhead and the service department manager gets a big cut. Go to an independent mechanic. Even the parts sold at dealerships are marked up."

I experimented with my own car and discovered that my neighbor knew what he was talking about. I saved $125.85 by going to an independent mechanic when I needed a new carburetor.

A friend took her car back five times to the dealership and they could never seem to fix it so it wouldn't stall in the middle of left-hand turns. Each time they told her it needed two or three other things fixed. She tried the same independent mechanic I use. Her car hasn't stalled since. All she needed was replacement of the automatic choke.

Another friend took her car in to have the brakes checked because they failed in heavy traffic. When they called her to pick up the car, the service manager said, "We couldn't find anything wrong with your brakes." The bill for inspecting her brakes was almost $100.

On the way home, her brakes failed again. She called all of her friends, pleading with them to recommend a good mechanic. He turned out to be only six blocks from her house. He made a minor adjustment in the brake lines and the bill was under $60. Her brakes have not failed since.

HOW TO AVOID BECOMING AN AUTO REPAIR VICTIM

The moral of the story is to ask every one of your friends about their mechanics and keep a handy list of names and telephone numbers. A good mechanic who can be trusted and doesn't overcharge because you don't understand cars or because you're a woman, is as valuable as a good nanny!

- Make sure your automobile legitimately needs repairs. It is surprising how often people take a car in for repairs that it does not need! Often it is "because of funny noise coming from underneath." Bend down as low as you can and *look* under your car. At least three times in my life I have found that my noise was a newspaper, a tumbleweed, or a paper box that I had snagged in traffic. A friend discovered that the bumping noise in the rear of her car wasn't a bearing but her spare tire moving around in the trunk.

- If your car is still running, but behaving in strange ways, it is wise to take it to an auto diagnostic center for analysis. If you belong to the American Automobile Association, they do theirs from a van that travels around. In their magazine you can discover when the van will be near your neighborhood.

  If you go to a diagnostic center that is also a repair station, then the advice is the same as looking for a surgeon. Most of these computer analyses cost under $50. Get diagnoses from two different places and then compare the print-outs. Pick the mechanic you trust the most. He may not necessarily be the cheapest.

- Don't contract to have a job done immediately. Check around. Even on highway off-ramps, if there is one station that does repairs, there are usually two or three. Walk around if you must to inquire.

- Ask the mechanic for his license and other identification. Gas stations and repair shops have them displayed on the office wall.

- If you have been towed to a suspicious repair shop, or feel that the quote seems out of bounds, call the Better Business Bureau or the State Licensing Board to see if the mechanic is licensed before you sign papers authorizing any work.

- If you are trying to save money by getting car repairs done by a mechanic who advertises in a free throw-away paper, especially check him out. There is a shortage of good mechanics, and those who have to advertise in such papers can't have a long list of satisfied customers lined up for their work. These ads also carry more nonlicensed workmen of all types.
- Ask for a written estimate.
- Never pay cash.
- Don't be fooled by a low price. It may mean that the mechanic is so poorly skilled that he is enticing business. It can also mean that he will quote a low price, and then discover all kinds of extra things that run the bill sky high once he has your car disassembled.

16

USED CAR TRICKS

All of the used car mishaps about to be related actually happened to friends or relatives of mine — and one happened to me.

THIS DEAL SMELLED FISHY

Sally was a widow, exhausted from a tension-filled day, when her 17-year-old son cornered her and told her he had saved enough to buy his first car. He wanted her to go with him to shop for the car. Sally knew about as much about cars as she did about race horses — which was nothing except that sometimes they ran.

She was as uneasy in the used car lots he took her to as she would have been walking around in a bordello. The salesmen quickly became aware of that.

Although her son, Ron, explained every time exactly how much money he had and what he was interested in, they always led him to cars that "your mom can help you finance."

Sally survived the first two used car lots in fairly decent shape. But at the third, an older man led them immediately to what he called a "cream puff." The car looked new.

"It belonged to an anesthetist at the hospital," the

salesman glibly explained, "and he had a sports car, too, so this one didn't get much use. You know how fastidiously neat doctors are about their cars."

No, she didn't know that. But it was obvious that whoever had owned this car had been nitty-picky.

The salesman popped the hood and then with a dramatic flourish said, "Will you look at that! He kept the engine steam cleaned all the time."

"It's exactly like new," Ron crowed. Sally began to have doubts. It looked to her like the entire engine and its compartment had been repainted just recently and all the wires looked very new.

While Ron experimented with the power brakes and windows, Sally asked, "Could you open the trunk? I want to see how many suitcases and things it will hold."

The salesman proudly popped the latch. "Five people could travel with ease in this pam-pered baby!"

While he returned to Ron, she pulled the new carpeting up in one corner and looked under it. RUST!

She pulled it back at the other corner and found even more rust. Then she went around the side and pulled a corner of the carpeting up behind the driver's seat — RUST!

The salesman and Ron were back bending over the engine compartment. She knelt down and reached up under the brake and pulled that carpet back — still more rust. She looked in the freshly painted glove compartment. Way in the back she found more rust.

"Why, this car has been in a big flood or in a river or lake for a long time. It's all rusty," she exclaimed. "Some insurance company must have paid it off as a total loss and then someone salvaged it."

"I beg your pardon," the salesman exclaimed. "We are a very honest, trustworthy firm. You are insulting us!"

"Then why does this car smell like dead fish?"

His eyes bulged as he stared at her. He reached up and scratched the top of his head. Instantly the loudspeaker paged his name. "I'm wanted in the office pronto," he said and left on the run.

She looked toward the office and saw the entire staff staring at her. "Come on, Ron, there's nothing here that you want." And she got back into her car and started the motor. Muttering and complaining, Ron got back in the car.

"I really liked that car," he grumbled all the way to the police station, where she filed a complaint. When the police went to the lot, the car had disappeared. No one there even knew which car the police were talking about.

"The lady must be confused. She wasn't at this place at all."

One week later a policewoman went to the same lot, inspected the same car, financed it and turned the paperwork, pictures of the car, and the car, over to the district attorney's office. Investigation proved that the car had indeed been under the water for quite some time. So had several other cars on the lot. Insurance companies had paid for their demise.

THE LATEST WORD IN TRANSPLANTS

Jim was getting old and tired. He wasn't as broke as he imagined he was, but he was frightened every time he spent any money. He had bought three very old used cars during the seven years since he retired and they had all died on him.

While waiting for a bus one day he began talking to the man who owned the Good News Used Cars lot right beside the bus stop. The owner was the only salesman.

"I used to cross-country haul. Had my own rig. Decided to sit still for a while," he explained. "So I'm doing this. I pick my cars out very carefully at the wholesale market. They are old, beat-up, sold 'as is,' but everyone of them runs well and is safe."

It sounded right to Jim so he quoted a price and asked the man to show him what he could afford to buy for that amount.

"Why this one! It still has lots of muscle and not too many miles on it. Not many dents either."

Jim circled it twice. It seemed to be priced cheap for the condition it was in. Even the upholstery was clean.

"Can I take it for a test drive?"

"Sure thing. Just leave your driver's license here with me for a warranty that you'll come back."

Jim drove it around the big block. It sounded good. The brakes grabbed the road quickly when he pressed them. It didn't rattle or shake. It steered straight.

He didn't know much more about cars than that. He decided to drive it about one mile further where the road went up a steep hill to see how it performed.

But before he reached the hill he drove past the 24-hour station with the mechanic's bay where he had taken every car he ever owned. He drove in. Joe, his favorite man, was on duty.

"How do you like this doll?" Jim asked.

"Are you kidding, Jim? You didn't buy that, I hope!"

Jim's face fell. "You don't like it? You didn't even ask the price."

Joe leaned in the open window and placed his hand on Jim's arm. "Friend," he said, "that isn't one car. You're driving two cars that have been cut in half and welded together after they were both totaled in some accident. The back end and front end don't even match. Even the wheel sizes are different!"

Jim scrambled out of the car. He adjusted his glasses and looked. Joe, he could see, was right. "It can't be fixed, can it?"

"Can a horse give birth to a calf? Look, Jim, let me find you a car. Sooner than later someone always comes in here with a car they want to unload. A car I've worked on, so I know its map and history."

Three months later Jim owned a car that had almost been repossessed. It was the cheapest car on the market, had a few dings in it, but it never gave him any trouble.

A "TOTAL" DISGUISE

Ruth was a mature secretary. She was starting her life over after age 50 and some pretty hard knocks in life. She was not experienced with cars but pretty sharp about a lot of things. She went to the beautiful showroom near her office where late model cars were traded in for shiny new models.

She hoped to snare a Honda or something good. Instead the salesman led her to a Colt.

"Not a dent in it!" That was true. She circled it. The car looked brand new, yet it was six years old.

She looked at the odometer. The mileage was low. The tires showed practically no wear. What else had her Dad told her on the phone last night? She bounced the right fender to see how strong the shocks were. Then she bounced the left fender.

She asked to go for a test drive. The salesman went along with her, talking all the while. The car ran well. It felt good. In fact she couldn't think of one reason why she shouldn't buy it.

While he was filling out the papers, she was reading the papers upside down. As a secretary she often did that while her boss was dictating. All of a sudden her eyes were glued to the registration papers.

"Where was this car for three years? Why does it list no owner for three years?"

"Ahhh. It was in storage. That's why the mileage is

so low."

"But even if it was in storage, wouldn't it have to be registered to an owner?"

"Not if it isn't being driven."

That puzzled her. Her brother, living in the same state as she did, had had to pay a small fee, not full registration, for the year he stored his car while he went to Europe.

"Who owned it last?"

"Ahhh. We bought it from storage. They hadn't paid their fee for the last year."

"Who was it insured with?"

The salesman, an older man, began to get annoyed. "Now look, miss, I can't fill out all these papers without making an error if you keep talking to me. Why don't you go get a free cup of coffee over there? There's also soft drinks and hot chocolate."

Ruth crossed the room, went out the side door and went back to the car. She opened the driver's door. There was not one service sticker pasted on it. For some reason she slipped her hand under the driver's seat and found an old letter, dated three years ago, caught in the carpeting. It had brown stains on it. She put it in her purse.

She went to the bathroom. Safe in a booth she opened the letter. It was from a parole officer. The owner of the car had missed one of his appointments. The county form letter listed the parolee's name, address, and case number. It also had the parole officer's name and telephone number. She put it back in her purse.

When she walked back to the salesman, he looked up and said, "Almost finished!"

She smiled wanly. "I'm feeling a bit ill. Would you mind if we finished this tomorrow?"

"But I can't promise to hold the car for you! It might be gone."

"Then that will mean that it wasn't meant for me, wouldn't it?"

"Well, maybe I could make some kind of arrangement. . ."

"Please excuse me. I really must go home. I feel very ill."

Without another word, without looking at him, without looking at the car, she walked straight to her car, climbed in, rubbed her forehead and drove off.

The next morning, she explained to the attorney she worked for what she had discovered at the car dealership.

"Should I call the sale off or what should I do?"

"Why don't you call the parole officer?"

Mr. Sidney, the parole officer, seemed surprised when she asked for his parolee. "Why, he was killed in a car accident three years ago. His car was totaled."

"Totaled?"

"Yes, AAA sent it to a junk yard to be crushed. Since he had no kin, I sort of followed his case to its final closing."

"Then you'd remember what his car looked like? The model and the year."

"Sure. It was a 1983, red two-door Colt hatchback."

"Well, it's powder blue now."

Having been so nearly burned, Ruth leased a car for the next year. By then she was able to buy a new car with her name on the registration slip as the original owner.

A BUNCO SALE WITH A HAPPY ENDING

Mariann was a divorced mother raising two young teenagers, neither of them old enough yet to drive. But her daughter was taking driver's education in high school. Their one and only car was a "smoker" and in their town you got tickets for smokers. She wouldn't be able to let Becky use it after she got her license.

So she went shopping in the classifed ads for a one-owner, distress sale, of an inexpensive car. She found one right away. It read: "low mileage. Well cared for."

She went to see it after work and liked everything about it including the nice young couple who were "reluctantly" giving it up.

It had a lot of safety extras, tires that were almost new. "I'll have to make arrangements for the loan from my credit union," she explained. "And they don't open until noon."

That was agreeable. She gave them a small down

payment and filled out the papers that they were going to take to the Department of Motor Vehicles the next day. The man said, "We have to go out of town for the weekend, so will it be all right if we deliver the car to you Sunday night after 9 P.M.?"

It was Thanksgiving week. The nights were dark. It was especially dark when they delivered the car on the Sunday night after Thanksgiving. They seemed such an honest couple. Along with the transfer papers, they gave her the complete service records on the car, which showed the engine and brakes to be "A-okay."

She didn't have much opportunity to look it over Monday, but she drove it to work. As she was getting out of the car, she pulled her purse out from behind the driver's seat where she always stashed her purse, and small pebbles of broken windshield glass fell on the cement.

At noon, she called them.

"Oh, don't worry about the glass. We thought we had it all swept out. Last New Year's Eve we parked it behind the theater while we were attending a film and some revelers threw a brick through the windshield.

"There was nothing in the car to steal. It was just vandalism. Our insurance company had the windshield fixed immediately."

That night, soon after Mariann arrived home, her sister called from a distant state, "Mother just died!"

Mariann had planned to drive home for Christmas

and had already laid out almost all that they would be taking with them for the trip. So they packed quickly and left to drive 2700 miles.

Since it was dark when they started out it wasn't until they stopped for breakfast in Arizona, after eleven continuous hours of driving, that the gas station attendant pointed out to them that their tires were all threadbare. All four of them.

Mariann had commented on the almost new tires on the car when she bought it. She was astounded to find that the "nice young couple" had switched tires before they delivered the car to her. Now she had to worry: what else did they switch or tamper with or remove?

She only had a few charge cards. "Where is the nearest Sears?" When he told her it was a 13-hour drive, she asked, "Will these tires make it?"

"Drive slow. Avoid holes in the road."

In Albuquerque they bought four new tires at Sears and had them put on the car.

She also had the car greased, oil changed, and checked out there. The manager came up to her.

"There's something funny about your car here. The door jam list of oil changes and the wear and tear on this car looks like it should read about 70,000 miles, not what your odometer says. Did you just buy it?"

Mariann reached in the glove compartment. "I still have all the papers here. The repairs, etc."

The kindly white-haired man studied the papers.

"Ma'am? What you have here is a used driver's education car. And I guessed about right. The last time it had its safety check it was at 69,000 miles."

Mariann paled. "My mother just died. I still have almost 2,000 miles to drive and then I have to drive back again. Will this car make it?"

Since the car was already raised, he went under it with a light. When he came back out he said, "In your state they are pretty strict on driver's education cars. This one has been well cared for. Have a good trip. You have nothing to worry about. But I would check with the Department of Motor Vehicles when you return. This could be called a *bunco sale*."

Mariann not only made the trip safely with no problems other than the tires, but she fell in love with that car, so much that she kept it for ten years and drove it for another 100,000 miles before she bought a new car.

The Department of Motor Vehicles did investigate and discovered that the former owners had deliberately thrown a brick through their windshield and smashed the dashboard so they could get a new odometer set at 0000. The car had never been driven faster than 35 miles an hour. It had never been in an accident.

PROTECT YOURSELF

- Consumer Reports advises that anyone buying a used car should have it checked by a trusted mechanic or take it to a good diagnostic center, such as the one run by AAA.

- If you are not driving the car home immediately, take along your camera and photograph the car inside and out. Get a written, signed agreement on what comes with the car — such as the tires!

- AAA advises that if you are selling your car, don't give a buyer the certificate of title until you have cashed his or her check.

- AAA warns you to be especially cautious if considering a car represented as "restored salvage" or offered at a ridiculously low price.

- They also advise that if you are buying a used car, protect yourself from getting a stolen vehicle.

To do this, if you are buying a car from a private party, or even a used car lot, always take a friend with you. In your pocket or purse carry a small notebook and pencil.

Have the friend be your stooge. While you snoop around the car, you friend should keep asking questions to keep the seller unaware of what you are doing.

Lift the hood. Inspect the engine and everything under the hood, then look up near the hood closing (On my car, on the left hand side of the body just above the engine).

There are two numbers there. The one in smaller black numerals is your car's registration number. The one above it, harder to read, engraved in the metal in larger letters and numbers is your body number. There is also a number on the engine, but you must know where to look for it. If either number seems to be rubbed out, painted over, tampered with — beware. If the paint around them seems newer than the rest of the paint, note that down, as you write down the numbers.

Tell the salesman you will come back after you think it over. Drive to the police station. Their computers often have a list of all known stolen cars from your state, nearby states and perhaps country-wide.

If you do buy a stolen car, you may end being forced to return it to its rightful owner and losing every penny you paid the thief.

17

PIES IN THE SKY AND PENNY STOCKS

Enticements are dangled like bait in some of the most reputable places. Local newspapers and *USA Today* run ads listed under "Capital Needed" or "Investors Wanted," captivating ads that stir your imagination. Want to own part of a real producing gold mine? Or an oil well that will never run dry? You can also invest in part ownership of a horse that is guaranteed to be a winner.

But most of them aren't worded that blatantly. If you call the number listed in the ad, one or two well-dressed, refined gentlemen driving an expensive late-model car will arrange to meet you for an 8:30 or 9 A.M. breakfast at a pleasant but not expensive restaurant.

One will state, "That is the only time we have free for the next few days." Translated, that means: "This is the cheapest meal we can buy and we can use the corner booth as our free office."

It also suggests, "We're overwhelmed with clients," which he knows will tickle your interest and avarice.

Then the pitch comes. The horse is a "sleeper" that they are keeping under wraps; they're only letting one or two people invest in its sure winnings.

The gold isn't exactly a mine. But it is real gold still in the earth. They may even show you some nuggets, let you examine them, even offer to go with you to have them appraised.

They may be peddling limited partnerships in oil or gas which they claim are not regulated by the SEC and therefore do not need to be registered.

Or they offer bargain stocks, called *penny stocks*, but fail to point out the big risks.

You stand to lose all of your investment in any and all of these pitched ventures but the promoters will lose nothing. They will just relocate somewhere else and work with some new schemes. They always find new pies to slice.

All of these ventures are looked upon by the state regulators and the Securities and Exchange Commission (SEC) as unregistered securities.

The seller will insist to you that such offerings are not regulated. He will also point out that he doesn't have to let you in.

If you're meeting in a restaurant, he will at that point make you anxious by asking for the check and preparing to leave. Or, if you are on the telephone, he may cut off your questions and arguments by hanging up the phone with the statement, "I was just trying to do you a favor!"

The con artist knows exactly when his victim has taken the bait. He knows your appetite will be whetted now and you will most likely follow through, because his apparent retreat makes you feel like you are being cheated out of something good. Within an hour, you will probably sign a check over to him, usually in a restaurant.

He is wrong about the SEC. Both state and federal regulators, wishing to protect investors, look upon these offers and many others as public securities that should be either registered or submitted to the regulators for an exemption.

Upon careful scrutiny you will find that the "gold" offer usually turns out to be processing gold tailings still left in the ground or in a pile of dirt. Naturally it will take two or three years of intensive screening to separate the gold from the dirt before the money can come pouring in to you. By that time the bird that thought up the scheme and your money will be long gone.

These offers can include investments in producing a movie, recording a rock band, magic new cosmetics or diet pills, expanding a small business, developing a resort. The sky is the limit on schemes.

But they all seem to be promoted in the same way: you are being offered a tempting "piece of the pie," to get in on the ground level of a "big deal" that promises to make a lot of money for you.

Examine the way the investments are promoted. If they promise earnings that are far above average, such as 18% return with no risk, be wary. The biggest returns come from the most risky investments.

The first step you should always take before investing in any of these ventures, or limited partnerships in gas or oil wells or other businesses, is to check out the offer by calling the SEC's Public Reference Branch telephone, (202) 272-7450, to find out if the offering is registered or has filed for registration. Documents on the offering, if registered or pending, are available for your scrutiny.

Another safety checkpoint is with your state's securities administrator. Call the North American Securities Administration Association, (202) 737-0900. They will direct you to your state's securities administrator, who will tell you if the offering is registered or exempt.

HOT SPOTS IN THE U.S.

Scam brokers even have their favorite watering holes where they sell specialized stock. In Las Vegas and Reno you can find them five deep hanging around the bars to catch suckers. If they call you cold on the telephone, ask them where they are calling from, and then study a map of the U.S. or Canada and you can tell where you will get burned with what kind of investments.

Vancouver and Calgary: mining stocks
Spokane: precious metals, mining stocks, penny
      stocks
Salt Lake City: penny stocks and blind pools
Denver: penny stocks, blind pools, oil and gas,
      precious metals
Minneapolis: junk bonds
Boston: precious metals and rare coins

New York: penny stocks, rare coins, precious
metals, blind pools
Nashville: oil and gas
Memphis: coal
Little Rock: coal and junk munis
Jackson: junk munis
Atlanta: oil and gas, foreign futures
Fort Lauderdale and Miami: precious metals,
penny stocks, oil and gas, newsletters
Tampa: penny stocks and junk munis
Gulfport: oil and gas
Dallas: oil and gas, precious metals
Scottsdale: real estate, precious metals
Las Vegas: precious metals, penny socks, mining
stock
Southern California: diamonds and gems, pre-
cious metals, rare coins, futures, strategic
metals, foreign futures, oil and gas

These are also the locations of telemarketing
boiler rooms, thick and fast-talking. As fast as they
are raided, they just move down the street.

PENNY STOCKS AND BLIND POOLS

You should know that these are not always scams,
unless you are not told in advance of the considerable risk, but they are always of a *highly* speculative
nature. They seem to catch many "penny-wise and
pound-foolish" people. They also appeal to low-in-
come people.

Penny stocks. New companies issue multi-million
shares at a very low price (perhaps under $2) to get

142

people to speculate. The companies usually have no financial backing and the people involved are not well known in financial circles. You have a tiny chance of breaking even on these, but don't hold your breath — you're in Fantasyland.

Blind-pool penny stocks. You do not know, in this case, what you are speculating on, and invest on faith in your broker or the pool manager.

Blind pool. This is a company shopping for some other business to buy. No business plans or details are provided because they have none yet. You just own a piece of something, but you don't know what it is and neither do they! In other words, the worst kind of a lottery.

Municipal bonds. Municipal bonds are bonds issued by cities when they need money to build a convention center, rejuvenate their downtown area, or for some other improvement. The advantage to municipal bonds is that they are federal, and sometimes also state, tax-free. The soundness of these bonds depends on the financial strength of the city. If the city is fighting bankruptcy, then they may be junk bonds, or *junk munis.* Back away!

ADVANCED FEE FRAUDS

These are "take the money and run" scams. Small businessmen, farmers and even large corporations get caught by them. Anyone who is in need of loan and having trouble getting it is bait. For an advanced fee you will be granted the loan "from a foreign bank whose identity must be kept secret."

Around the world people have been ripped off by this one, even foreign governments, for example Zambia.

The typical victim is a small businessman who needs to borrow $500,000 but has been turned down by several legitimate lenders. The advance fee on such a deal would be from $25,000 to $50,000. The fee is paid, but the loaned money never appears.

18

LEGAL RAIDERS ON YOUR SAVINGS

The U.S. Government tries to plug up the gaps used by legal raiders, but almost every minute of every day some shrewd mind thinks of a new gimmick to poke a hole in the dike.

Some of these scams involve mutual funds, junk bonds and limited partnerships. None of these are scams in themselves. They become scams when someone asks you to purchase these products without pointing out the risks involved in each.

Contrary to folklore tales, good investments aren't often playing hunches. Investments must be based on good sound research. They must be well thought out.

Sometimes, well-established brokerage houses, as we have recently learned, can't be trusted to do this research for us. It's our job to protect our own money by keeping ourselves informed.

JUNK BONDS
The term *junk bonds* is professional jargon for high yield-low quality bonds that have no Standard and Poor's or Moody rating.

They remain a good, often high yield investment,

as long as the issuer can pay the interest or dividends. Unfortunately, there is no guarantee that this will happen. Since these junk bonds are usually issued to pay for a company takeover, or a leveraged buy-out, the issuing company is in deep debt with an uncertain future at the outset. The company must pay back the bonds and also earn a profit — the holders of the bonds can win big or lose big. The junk bonds can't fly until the business in question takes off. If they are wiped out by bankruptcy your bonds become just what they are called: junk.

WARNING

If an investor uses a broker, the law requires the broker to read a warning to the investor before issuing junk bonds.

The warning beings: "As a potential investor, you should understand that there is an important inverse relationship between the management of a fund's principal value and interest rates. When interest rates rise, principal value declines."

The statement goes on to explain that in recent months the risk has increased significantly. Recessionary times bode ill for junk bonds. When the economy is growing and the bond issuer's company is thriving, then junk bonds can be a somewhat better investment.

Brokers may not pitch high income-low quality bonds. They can inform, point out all the pros and cons, but they must let you decide for yourself if you want to take the risk. You can't say the broker didn't warn you.

History has proven many junk bonds to be very poor risk investments that have cost people their fortunes. Junk bond scams have recently been big news.

The American Association of Retired People advises its members not to take risks with their money after age 60. By that age they advise that the bulk of your money should be invested in conservative funds that generate income for retirement. They recommend a mutual-fund portfolio.

AARP points out that at this age the temptation is always there to reach for high risk or bad investments. Older people think it is their last chance to double their money. This is one reason they get taken so often.

MUTUAL FUNDS

Mutual funds are investment companies that invest money from large numbers of shareholders in a wide spectrum of companies or industries. At the time of this writing, 30 million people have more than $1 trillion invested in 2,000 mutual funds.

The goal of some mutual funds is long-term capital gain; others aim for individuals who need a steady flow of income. Investors nearing or at retirement age need to buy mutual funds that invest in utilities that pay high dividends, high-grade corporate bonds and various government bonds. They pay a better interest rate, for instance, than treasury bills or money market funds.

While the return on mutual funds over the last ten years hasn't been as high as the stock market (270.41 percent according to the Standard and Poor 500 Index) it has come in at 207.22 for the same period and with less risk.

If you are thinking of investing in mutual funds, the most important factor is the past performance of the fund over many years. Study the prospectus carefully. Also remember that 30% of junk bonds are held by mutual funds; these may not be the funds for you. The Securities and Exchange Commission requires that these prospectus reports give you the whole picture, not just a semi-annual report that you can't compare to anything else. You need to see what the fund did last year and the years before and how it compared to other mutual funds. Only then should you make your decision.

NO-LOAD FUNDS

Another important consideration is whether or not the fund is a *no-load* fund. The American Association of Retired People as well as many experts all recommend that you choose such a fund.

A no-load fund charges about 0.5 percent per year for management. Printings, mailings, customer services and distribution take out another .05 percent. These charges, totaling about 1 percent of the assets, are subtracted from the fund's earnings before distribution is made to the investor.

There is no brokerage fee to pay because there is no broker or account manager working with you.

No-load accounts are bought, sold and moved from one account to another by telephone or mail. You may shuffle your funds from one type of account to another without additional charge.

With a no-load fund, you must think things out and make your decisions on your own. Then you can call a representative of the fund and state what you want to invest and where. The person you talk to cannot legally give you any advice, and only takes your orders. You are your own driver.

LOAD FUNDS

A *load* account, which is a regular brokerage account, charges you for everything you do. If you move money from one account inside your mutual fund into their money market account, for example, there is a charge. The load can run from 4 to 8.5 percent. Some load funds also charge you a fee when you redeem your shares.

People on fixed incomes often find the movement charges intimidate them into keeping all their money in lower earning money market accounts, which allow check writing privileges, instead of moving funds for the greatest advantage.

LIMITED PARTNERSHIPS

In the early 80s, a favored investment known as a limited partnership appeared on the scene. It was promoted as a high risk investment structured to provide varying degrees of tax relief and income. Many limited partnerships were designed to lose money in order to provide tax shelters for individuals. Some of these partnerships defrauded the investors, and many seemed like outrageous tax evasion. When the tax laws changed, money-losing limited partnerships no longer provided tax benefits and thus faded from the scene.

But other types of limited partnerships are still plentiful.

The limited partnership is set up by a management team called the general partners to accumulate funds for an investment, which may be real estate, oil, mining, container rental, television cable, or countless other ventures. Shares of the partnership are sold to investors, called limited partners.

Partnerships are often structured to pay out a certain percentage of interest and principle on a regular basis, and the venture may be sold at the end of the partnership period, perhaps ten years. The proceeds of the sale are then distributed to the limited partners. There are often tax advantages, although smaller than in years before the Simplified Tax Act.

For the creation and management of the limited partnership, the general partners charge a percentage of all money invested by the limited partners.

There are problems, aside from the considerable risk involved. Often only the general partner is sure of making money from such a set-up. Most partnerships do not provide liquidity: that is, you cannot convert your investment to cash, and you cannot sell your shares. Because of the risky nature of limited partnerships, you cannot borrow against your investment.

Limited partners sometimes get taken because of their over-eagerness and lack of investigation. Thoughtful investors should check to see how much of their own money the general partners will invest in the project. From this information and the investor's estimate of their charges, the investor could judge what is at risk for the general partners. The less risk for them, usually the larger the risk for the limited partners.

Check the performance of other partnerships the general partners have participated in. Try to contact some of the limited partners to ask your questions directly. Find out if other partnerships have switched within the term of the partnership from income generation to growth. In that case, the investor's disbursements are withheld and used to purchase more assets for the partnership. This can leave some investors who need the income in a poor financial situation.

HUNDREDS OF THOUSANDS LOST

In Oregon, a corporate president set up a limited partnership to enable the corporation to fund a new venture. When his corporation began to have financial difficulty, the corporate president, who was the general partner, began siphoning off funds from the limited partnership to shore up his corporation. At the same time, he leaked information which caused the stock value of the corporation to rise sharply. He sold his stock for a large sum, the corporation declared bankruptcy, and the limited partners lost fortunes.

Who gained? Of course he did, because of the sale of his stock. And so did the brokers who sold the partnerships, the accountants, and the lawyers, who came in at the end to clean up the mess.

A TRULY LEGAL SCAM

Tax credits and long term tax relief have traditionally been the means by which the federal government stimulates investment into such worthy projects as low income housing and alternate forms of energy. But the federal government is by its very nature political, and political pressure can at any time put an investment at risk.

And so it happened to thousands of investors in 1986 when the federal government passed the Simplified Tax Act, which eliminated limited partnerships as tax shelters. This removed the benefits which large and small investors alike had expected from their money. This legal scam lost investors millions of dollars.

STOCK MARKET SCAMS

When the stock market made its historical correction in October 1987, those who didn't keep an eye on their accounts or couldn't get through the telephone jam found they were the biggest losers. Some brokers advised clients to sell, reinvest, move stocks and bonds from one account to another. Other brokers, who had not been granted a totally free hand in managing the accounts, just did it.

It wasn't until the phones were clear and the damage was done that some customers discovered their brokers had not cleared moves with them per agreement, or advised them of large losses, until their portfolios were greatly reduced in value.

Sometimes this shuffling was for no other reason than that each time the portfolio's contents resold or moved, the broker reaped an additional fat brokerage fee. Law suits are still pending on some of these scams. According to newspaper reports, many of the brokers and account executives who repeatedly took unnecessary risks are no longer in that profession.

Sound advice from good brokers is to go for "the long ride" and ignore the ups and downs. Pick good stock in a stable, growing company and ride along with it. Buy into the market when it is down and eventually it will go back up. In the end you will come out a winner and have lost little money in transfer fees. Your capital gains tax may be lower too, as you only pay it when you sell stock.

SAFE HAVENS

There is no risk-free investment, unfortunately. Even government insured accounts will change, if we can believe the news media, from guarantees of $100,000 per account to $100,000 *per person*, regardless of the number of his accounts.

you can still put your money in investments have the lowest possible risk. U.S. Treasury bills, U.S. savings bonds, Ginny Maes and money markets all pay lower interest rates than other, riskier investments. But they pay more than a bank savings account or interest-paying checking account.

SEND FOR INFORMATION
If you have any complaints, or suspect that your portfolio is being mismanaged by your account executive, you can report the problem to:

The Securities and Exchange Commission
Investor Complaints
Office of Consumer Affairs and
Information Services
450 5th Street, NW
Washington, DC 20549

All of the following Federal General Services Administration booklets can be obtained from:

Consumer Information Center-P
P.O. Box 100
Pueblo, CO 81002

Investment Swindles: How They Work and How To Avoid Them is a free booklet which tells you how to spot illegal investment schemes and how to protect yourself against legitimate sounding telemarketing and direct mail offers. No. 561-W.

Investors' Bill of Rights contains tips to help you make an informed decision on investment risks and costs. Free. No. 562-W.

Recent retirees who have had little practice or information in making investments can safeguard and improve their retirement years by sending for a comprehensive guide entitled *Managing Your Personal Finances.* This is presented in three parts, designed for use in a three-ring binder. they must be ordered as separate items.

Part 1. *The Principle of Managing Your Finances* tells how to assess your current financial status, set goals, develop a budget, carry it out, make adjustments. Includes foldout worksheets. 43 pages. No. 163W. Price $3.25.

Part 2. *Financial Tools Used in Money Management* tells how to use savings, investments, insurance, and credit to best achieve your financial goals. 22 pages. No. 164W. Price $1.50.

Part 3. *Coping With Change* contains worksheets and guidelines for responding to changes like retirement, inflation, unemployments, etc. 25 pages. No. 165W. Price $1.75.

One more booklet, *Money Matters,* offers tips for selecting the best financial planner, tax preparer, real estate broker, or lawyer at an agreeable price. 13 pages. No. 446W. Price $.50.

The price of each booklet is the cost of printing and distribution by the Government Printing Office.

19

TRAVELING?
ARE YOU SURE?

At the time of this writing, the Gulf crisis has thrown traveling into a quandary. No one is sure whether to plan a trip, especially by plane. Many have canceled all their travel plans. Major airlines are going bankrupt or merging.

Those airlines left are desperate to fill all their empty seats. They are again offering "two for one" (wife or friend flies free with a full-paying passenger) and reduced fare specials.

Judging by the overwhelming first response to these ads, it may again lead to overbooking, a disease that has plagued disappointed travelers for years, who arrive at the airport and find their flight filled or canceled.

FREQUENT FLIER OVERKILL

Airlines are also again giving double mileage credit for flights, which can be accrued for later free flights. There is a possibility that when tension in the Middle East eases, this practice will again bring back the frequent flier scam.

By 1990 these free promotional tickets had developed into "getting nowhere fast" or "nowhere at all." Travel scams, tour scams, frequent flier scams and free tickets can get people stranded.

The problem arose from the mushrooming of awarding free flights to encourage loyalties to certain airlines. Often business people accrue these flights while making business trips.

The airlines can only afford to allocate so much space to free flights. They must to depend on the paying passengers filling the plane to keep it flying.

To get a free or reduced fair flight during the few winter periods when air flight is down, it is necessary to make reservations months in advance. Summer travel is almost completely ruled out.

Some travelers benefit from the programs by taking free tickets and hotel stays in less popular destinations during off season.

The discounted and frequent flier tickets offered since the Gulf crisis seem to fit this pattern. However, many flight destinations no longer are offered. Schedules are thinner. There are fewer airlines operating. All this could mean your chances of using a frequent flier award to the destination you want have become even more slim.

TOUR SCAMS

Some tour operators default on tours, leaving travelers stranded in far-away places with empty pockets and a real case of the blues. Rising oil prices effect the travel industry. The falling dollar, the end of some airlines, and tours booking far in advance are other causes. Some are scams from the word "go."

If you are planning to take a trip, tour, or cruise, don't sign up with a company because of a bargain ad in a newspaper. Stick with the old faithfuls who have been in business for a long time and have a good reputation. The extra dollars spent may turn out to be many dollars saved!

FABULOUS VACATIONS

These offers seem to come to everyone, usually in your junk mail. Sometimes they are elaborately personal. "You have been especially named as a person deserving to join our deluxe exploration cruise to . . ."

The letter will be filled with tempting words about deluxe accommodations, free meals, celebrities who will be on the trip.

Your mouth will water over the colorful meals in the enclosed brochure, and the hotel or stateroom pictures will make you want to move in right now. The views, of course, are spectacular. The price is unbelievable.

Many of these brochures arrive in the mail with the announcement: "Congratulations. You have just won. . ." Others come over the telephone. "You've just been selected for a free week in Florida at. . ." The only requirement is that you must submit your credit card number to claim your trip, or send in a deposit to cover the port dues and other small fees to reserve your space on a cruise ship.

Many problems have come about since airline deregulation. There are some positive effects: it has

158

saved travelers over $100 billion, increased passenger loads by 50 percent and boosted the number of passenger miles flown by 65 percent.

But it unleashed travel scam operators who preyed upon consumers' desires to seek out legitimate bargains in the marketplace. Scams have been especially cruel to Americans who wish to visit relatives in Far East countries.

When deregulation occurred, airfares and travel prices increased and decreased into a bewildering morass. Even well-seasoned travel agents couldn't decipher the best bargains that might only be momentarily anyway. There was no way to compare which was the best price for a trip to Europe, for instance. The next day the prices might be completely different.

WHEN ABROAD — BARGAIN!

Americans are often too "nice" when they are abroad and therefore get used as suckers. Especially in Third World countries, the price asked is only meant to be the launching point for an exciting game.

In Asia, Africa, Latin America, and Southern Europe the rule is to offer just one half of the asking price and then rise in small increments until you reach a reasonable compromise.

To know what a reasonable price is, look in many shops before you make an offer on anything. Decide how much you will pay, and don't let yourself be haggled above that.

Don't buy anything on your first day out, or ever in big cities. Make your purchases in small villages where the sellers see fewer tourists and may be fairly honest.

Never go shopping with a guide. He'll steer you to all the most expensive things because he will collect a commission on what you buy.

A big rule for bargaining: never look impressed. The merchant will have the affair in his hands if you do. If you just shrug and walk on, he may call you back with a lower offer.

SURVIVING CUSTOMS

This advice may prevent *you* from committing fraud. Since October 1989, going through customs has been a little bit more hazardous, especially for absent-minded people.

Customs changed the guidelines defining *fraud* and *gross negligence* as those terms are used in civil penalty cases under Section 592 of the Tariff Act of 1930, as amended by a Treasury Decision and published September 6, 1989 in the *Federal Register.*

They eliminated the former requirement that to find fraud, Customs had to prove intent to defraud or otherwise violate the laws of the United States.

The new definition reads: "A violation is determined to be fraudulent if the material false statement or act in connection with the transaction was committed (or omitted) knowingly, i.e. was done voluntarily and intentionally, as established by clear and convincing evidence."

160

Gross negligence is now defined: "A violation is determined to be grossly negligent if it results from an act or acts of commission or omission done with actual knowledge of or wanton disregard for the relevant facts and with indifference to or disregard for the offender's obligations under the statute."

My darling globe-trotting Aunt Lu, who has left this world, was frequently in trouble with Customs for not listing something which she honestly did forget. She was once put off a ship and held overnight to settle a dispute over a purchase she had made in Holland on her first day, and forgotten when she left the country. It was a dainty, embroidered linen dress for a great grandniece. She placed it in the bottom of one of her suitcases under clothes she didn't need to wear while in Holland "because she wanted to keep it fresh."

AVOID TRAVEL PROBLEMS

ASTA (The American Society of Travel Agents) offers a booklet: *Avoiding Travel Problems.* It outlines nine warning signals to look for when a travel offer seems too good to be true. For a free copy, write;

ASTA
P.O. Box 23992
Washington, DC 20026-3992

The Council of Better Business Bureaus publishesa booklet entitled *Have You Won A Vacation?* which offers general information on "free" vacation certificates. For a copy, send a check or money order for $1 and a self-addressed, stamped envelope to:

Council of Better Business Bureaus
1515 Wilson Blvd.
Arlington, VA 22209

If you have already been a victim of one of these scams — mailed them a reservation check, or given them your credit card number — you can take the following actions:

First, write or call the company and try to cancel.

If you put the trip on a credit card, immediately contact the issuing bank by calling the number on the back of the bank statement; notify them of the incident.

The Federal Fair Credit Billing Act gives consumers 60 days from the date they receive the bill to put any dispute in writing. They should then mail the claim to the card issuer. If the consumer exercises his rights within those 60 days, the creditor can't take action against the consumer for not paying the bill until the dispute is resolved, and the consumer isn't obligated to pay for the item until the investigation has been completed.

However, scam artists often build in time frames to get around the 60-day billing provision by making it 12 months or more before you can select your travel dates, most of which will turn out to be unavailable.

When disputing a charge, always make photo copies of all documents, contracts and travel brochures, as well as all correspondence sent to the company, creditor or any other institution or agency to whom you complain. Be sure to use the account reference number on your credit card statement.

Since the victims of these scams seldom report them, there are no statistics to show how many people "bite."

SHADY CAMPSITE SALES

For those who do their traveling on a more modest scale and use recreational vehicles, a big new scam is in the selling of campsite spaces.

First, you receive a letter that invites you to visit the campgrounds and receive something like a Buick free if the lucky number on your letter matches the lucky number on the bulletin board. Even if you don't win the car, the letter guarantees you will win two or three other listed prizes.

They treat you like royalty when you arrive. A salesperson takes you into a booth and runs through a rapid sales talk. They show you slides or brochures of their wonderful campgrounds. You jump as a whistle or bell rings and the salespeople clap and cheer.

"What's that?"

"Another lucky person has signed up to join our happy family!"

For some people, owning a membership in a private campground (which can resemble a country club) is a great idea. And many of them are happy that they joined.

But an estimated half million people who have

purchased memberships at some 600 private campgrounds during the last 30 years regard it as a scam. Too often they were high-pressured into making the purchase on the spot. "This price is only for today, for this guest visit!"

These people have found that the memberships are far too overpriced unless they camp almost every weekend of the year. Then it gets boring to always go to the same place. Only on their vacations can working families use the choicer, more distant camps.

Often they find that the private campground is just as crammed as a public RV camping ground. They were promised more privacy space around their recreational vehicle. It fails to be there. All night, long distance campers are driving in, searching for their spaces.

Even though reservations must be made in advance and one stay can be no longer than two weeks, there are campers who must move back and forth between two camps. They regard themselves as regulars. They reserve the best spots.

The crowding in of the hugh RVs — some as large as Greyhound buses and others called "fifth-wheelers" — destroys all sense of camping in the woods. Some of these big jobs have large satellite antennas on their roofs.

For peace and privacy the woods-loving camping family must leave their unit and hike into the woodlands that surround these parks. Often the woodlands are part of a state park or national forest.

In some cases, Saturday nights are "Jamboree" and "game" nights, noisy and not whata true camper wants. On Sunday afternoons the "regulars" hold flea markets.

In other cases, glowing improvements are never made. Almost any newspaper — senior, church, free throw-away — or outdoor magazine contains a number of "lifetime camping memberships for sale — *half price.*"

In many cases the membership was purchased by a young family as a safe place for children to play and camp. In other cases it was picked by a retired couple in thier "quiet years." But more and more these parks are being filled with expensive rigs, or carabans of RVs that travel together to party loud and late.

What was promised to many, the very ones who struggle the hardest to pay their membership, was not delivered. This is the scam.

There is no nationwide organization that keeps statistics on campground memberships and those who purchase them. Many state governments are beginning to.

Virginia, Florida, Michigan, Colorado and Texas Better Business Bureaus are reaching the "alarmed" condition. In these states, they have instituted a cooling off period of three to five days (not counting weekends or holidays) during which the purchaser of a campground membership can send the company a certified letter canceling the contract.

SHOPPING FOR A CAMP

Thousand Trails, Inc., is the largest of the members-only campgrounds. Their top-of-the-line membership entitles members and their families unlimited use (up to two weeks per visit) of all current and future campgrounds. This lifetime membership, which can be willed to two generations, costs $7,500. Term memberships are $3,500. For either membership there are annual dues which range between $250 and $300.

At other campgrounds such as Outdoor World, Park Homes, Inc. or Ski and Sea, term or lifetime memberships range from $2,000 to $11,000.

Members-only campgrounds are affiliated with one or two reciprocal-use organizations: Coast to Coast and RPI. Coast to Coast charges an annual fee of $29 for people who want to stay in cabins. RPI charges $40 per year. Members of either organization then pay a fee of $1 or $2 per night at the campground to bring in their RVs.

A majority of those who belong to the reciprocal camp memberships claim they really enjoy them as they offer a quality of camping rarely equaled by campsites open to the general public.

Before you buy:

- Ask for a complimentary weekend to try it out.
- Talk to other members who have lifetime

memberships.

- Inspect all amenities (swimming pool, tennis courts, fishing ponds, etc.) closely. If they don't exist now, ask for proof that a surety bond has been posted with the state to ensure their construction.

- Read the sales contract carefully. Verbal promises carry no legal weight.

- Contact the Better Business Bureau in that area to see if there have been complaints.

- Give yourself time to think it over. If the salesperson high-pressures you, "It's this price only if you buy today," walk out. In one case, a couple asked to take the sales literature with them to study while they thought it over. They were not allowed to take the literature out of the building!

- Don't buy it as an investment. Buy it because you love to camp and intend to use it often.

20

CONTRACTORS AND HOME REPAIR SCAMS

Ask ten different people who have used contractors for any purpose in the past few years and almost half of them will groan with agony. Of the others, one or two will rave, "I couldn't have survived without him!" The rest will shrug their shoulders. "The job was finally completed and mostly we are satisfied."

Why this discomfort with contractors? One reason is that contractors too often get their licenses by going to school and do not rise up through the ranks of their trade. How can a person who has never built a house or anything else become a building, roofing, or remodeling expert?

The current way is for a bright person to study the right books and pass the general contractor's license exam. Then he seeks out and hires a man with years of experience in the field and licensed as a supervisor. From this point on the contractor will only be seen occasionally on jobs doing a "drive-by" inspection. This is all legal.

The contractor then rides around in an expensive car, wears high-priced suits to impress you with his success and talks you into giving him your business.

He has the manners of a chief executive. He talks like an attorney. He looks honest. He knows all the right words. He books jobs all day and all week long. He demands payment, usually one half or one third of the total estimate, in advance, before his crew will start the job. You are then a fly caught in a spider web!

He hires more superintendents with proper licenses and soon he has more jobs with completion dates agreed upon than he can possibly fulfill. So what does he do? He has his superintendent hire men from the casual labor markets, sometimes right off street corners, often men who can't even communicate with each other in the same language. He has these minimum wage crews start the job.

They tear your house apart, usually the kitchen or a bathroom, sometimes the roof or your front driveway, and then the workmen can disappear for weeks or months because they are starting another job which they will also leave waiting while they start new jobs.

The problem increases because there is a very serious shortage of skilled, licensed, housing contractors in this country. In California, court records show that there are at least 200,000 — but perhaps twice that many — unlicensed contractors preying upon homeowners.

DISASTER TERMITES

Every time part of the country is declared a "disaster area" and government loans are available for repairs, these slimy menaces come crawling out from under the rocks. They descend from all corners of the country on the stricken area just like miners on a gold rush.

You wake up to the sound of hammers tapping on the frame of your house or the foundation. You are getting a "free inspection" and are about to receive a "free estimate." They hand you a printed card (it only takes an hour to get a supply of business cards printed) that reads: "All of our work is guaranteed." There will be a license number on it.

But unless you check out that license number with the Contractor's Licensing Board, business license registrations, or some other authority in your locale, it could easily be their truck or boat license number, a telephone number picked at random or a dog, hunting or fishing license number.

The October 17, 1989 California earthquake attracted these "termites" from all over the country. California State's Contractors License Board cracked down on violators and processed more than 28,000 complaints in 1990.

HOME REPAIR SCAMS

In one outrageous scam an elderly San Jose, California woman was having trouble with her apartment furnace when the con man knocked on her door and said he was there to check it. After she admitted him, he warned her not to turn the furnace on as there was a gas leak in it. It would cost $600 to repair.

When she told him she'd have to call her landlord first and have him okay the bill, the man said he'd do it for her. He made a call, pretended to talk to her landlord, told her the landlord okayed the job. He said the landlord promised to reimburse her.

After writing up a contract on his business stationery, he had her sign it. Then he insisted he would only do the job for cash. Since she didn't have $600 in the house but had just deposited her Social Security check, he drove her to the bank while she withdrew the money. Then he took the $600 and drove off to get the parts. She never saw him again.

Utilities companies around the country warn that the arrival of cold weather brings this kind of scam artist knocking at the doors of elderly people.

Police everywhere advise people to never let anyone into their homes without proper identification. Make them wait outside the door. Then call the utility, or the company they claim sent them to make repairs in your house or apartment.

PLUMBER PIRATES ABOUND!

Home inspectors continually warn homeowners to be on the lookout for plumber pirates. These unscrupulous unlicensed plumbers, known in the field as "moonlighters," prey most often upon older people. They reap rich harvests and almost always leave behind a painful, expensive experience. However, the inspectors report that it's a rare plumber who's a pirate.

The problem is that when you have a plumbing problem it seems as urgent as an earthquake. You react without much thought. Cases pulled from the files of home inspection companies revealed many sad tales.

A water heater sprang a large spurting leak in the middle of the night. Flooding water in the basement threatened electrical appliances. The 81-year-old homeowner frantically called plumbers listed in a neighborhood free newspaper. Each time an answering machine took his message.

The live voice that answered agreed to be there within 20 minutes. The homeowner was too upset to ask to see his license. Once the electricity was shut off, and the hot water heater disassembled on the wet floor, the pirate plumber quoted an exorbitant price for repair.

Aghast, the homeowner stuttered that he didn't have that much money. The plumber asked how much he did have. He left with a check that wiped out the homeowner's checking account.

An aging woman living in a severe drought water-rationed area was bilked by a pirate plumber. He contracted to repair a leak in her toilet and replace the tank with a water-saving model.

While doing to work he said he found a hole in her house that needed to be fixed and dry rot in the bathroom floor. He needed a prepayment of $3,000 for labor to make these repairs.

He removed her toilet and most of the bathroom

floor. He took careful measurements. He wrote out an estimate of materials needed and said that would require another $1,800.

Since she used a walker and had only one bathroom, she was anxious to get the work finished. She wrote out the second check and asked him to try to finish the job before the day was over.

"No problem!" he said as he drove off to get the lumber and materials. He never came back. When she called the telephone number on his contract, she learned it didn't exist. The police found no licenses of any kind listed under his name.

A licensed plumbing contractor replaced the toilet with the newer model but found no evidence of dry rot or a hole. He relaid the old flooring.

Unsuspecting victims have been known to pay up to $2,000 for a new laundry tub that costs about $100. They have also been charged $2,000 for a new basement toilet that should have been $150.

A GOOD PLUMBER

Since prices vary even among licensed plumbing contractors, it is always a good idea to take the time to get three estimates before hiring a job done.

In a moment of panic, when you need a plumber at the 11th hour, it is wise to already have on hand, in an easy-to-find place, the 24-hour telephone number of a plumber whose license and references you have already checked.

HOW CAN YOU TELL THE GOOD GUYS FROM THE BAD GUYS?

Honest business people approach you by running ads in the paper or the Yellow Pages, or are recommended by friends. You approach them while you see them on the job. Some out-of-work home repair workers come from out of state, but they bring credentials that can be checked out.

Scam home repairmen use strange language that you can't translate. "Your bathroom outlet isn't the GFCI type. It could cause a fire." They don't test it with a voltage meter. They don't seem to be carrying their tools right now.

They run a tape across your floor, bend down and look up at your walls. They do not use a plumb rule. "Gawd, but your walls are way out of plumb! That's dangerous, y'know?"

They walk along your foundation. Follow it all the way around the house. It looks okay to you but they keep shaking their heads. "Your foundation has endured 'hydrostatic lifting' that needs to be fixed for sure, first thing!"

Out comes the clipboard and they begin to write down figures, scratch heads, confer with each other, present you with an estimate. "If I were you, I'd want to get started on this right away before it gets worse!"

You stare unbelieving at the bottom line of the estimate. You do not observe or write down their make of car, color, license number or a description of them. But you do make a telephone call because you want to be reassured. You call the telephone number on the card. A very professional woman answers with the name of the firm.

"Why, yes, sir, our men are in your neighborhood this morning. You want references? I can give you a dozen right off." She starts spieling them off so fast you can't write them down. That wife or girl friend can really talk fast!

WHAT PROTECTION DO YOU HAVE?

- Do not sign with the first contractor you call in for an estimate, no matter how charming or convincing he is. Be especially wary if the bid sounds too low to be true. Always interview three contractors, get their written estimates and then spend several days thinking them over before you make the choice.

- Ask for the names, addresses and telephone numbers of people who have used this contractor. Do not just call these people. Ask if you may drop in and see the work for yourself. Chat with them. Find out if they have any grievances. Ask a nearby neighbor at random. The telephone contact could be a "set-up." Neighbors usually are willing to tell all they observed and to be impartial.

- Never meet with a contractor to discuss a job immediately after you have returned from work and have not yet eaten dinner! When you have low blood sugar because of fatigue and skipping a meal, believe it or not, your mind is sluggish, easily confused. These contractors know that and try to catch you with your energy down.

- Never part with any of your money until you have a contract which states, in addition to detailing the work to be done, the exact completion date. Agree to pay the final payment only after the work has passed local legal inspection and your satisfaction. If the up-front money asked for is more than one-third, be very suspicious. You may never see him or your money again — *or* get the work done.

- If the contractor is subcontracting any of the work, be sure to have it written in the contract that the subcontractors are to submit their bills directly to you and that *you will pay each one of them.* This is because of the Mechanics' Lien Law. If, after you have paid a contractor in full for satisfactorily completing the work on your property, he has not paid his subcontractors and cannot be located to pay them, under this law the subcontractors can demand payment from you; in lieu of payment they can place a Mechanics' Lien against your property. Either way, you end up paying twice for the work performed.

21

UNREAL
REAL ESTATE DEALS

The largest purchase that the average person makes in his lifetime is his home. Therefore it should be approached with great caution and preparation.

Buyers should do much studying before they go to a real estate agent. They should be sure what they want to spend, where they want to live and what kind of house they want.

This house usually becomes their best asset. It provides them with a place to live and a chance to build an estate through equity. Often it occupies a large part of their heart.

For these reasons, the purchase and the resale of a home are important moments in the life of most people. For young people, there is the "starter house," the first step to the home large enough to raise a family or provide the social setting they desire. For older people, the equity in their house provides for the comfort of their old age.

Unfortunately, during the late 80s the buying and selling of houses was not accomplished with as much thoughtful planning as it deserved. In many parts of the country it was almost panic buying. The real estate market was on such a steep climb that buyers thought they had to make a quick offer or lose the house. This was abetted by real estate salesmen who emphasized that to loiter was to lose.

There was no time for seriously studying the house, its location, its assets or its flaws. Realtors preached that if you didn't like it, you could always sell it within a year or so and make a big profit.

Homes were often appraised far beyond their reasonable value. Still, real estate agents urged buyers not to let the purchase slip away from them.

Now, at the time of this writing, the country is in a recessionary period and throughout the country real estate has dropped, on average, 20 percent in value.

The result is that approximately 10 percent of these overpriced houses, townhouses, and condos are in foreclosure. Since they required large down payments, this is destroying retirement dreams of older people. It is also dashing the hopes of young people. Many are forced into bankruptcy.

Suffering the most are the couples who put a down payment on a retirement home and depended on the sale of their present home. Sometimes they are paying on two mortgages. In other cases they must rent out the retirement house.

Others lost their down payment with their dreams and will remain in their present home. The reduced price of their present home, now worth approximately 20 percent less than in August 1989, doesn't provide enough equity for the move.

If you are a buyer, now is a good time to buy.

Whatever steps you take, use caution. Keep your eyes and ears alert for any scams.

MORTGAGE TRANSFERS

Be alert for this potential scam, which has occurred often enough to instigate government investigation.

You signed up for a mortgage on your house with one firm, but often the mortgage is sold to another company. You receive a letter informing you to stop sending your monthly checks to the local lender who provided you the mortgage. Now you must send it instead to another firm, hundreds or thousands of miles away.

The U.S. Government Accounting Office has found that transfers of mortgage servicing rights nearly doubled between 1985 and 1988 — up from $80 billion to $150 billion.

The new mortgage holder may demand higher payments per month to fill alleged escrow account deficits; or record keeping errors may occur. Many borrowers have complained that because of the transfers, their local property taxes and hazard insurance payments weren't made, exposing them to foreclosure or risk of huge uninsured losses.

Watch for a very slick fraud. A businesslike letter arrives, informing you that from now on your mortgage payment is to be sent to the address on the letterhead. The crooks may cash your check before you realize that you have been taken — and you still owe the mortagage payment to the actual mortgage holder.

In Colorado, a fictitious savings institution persuaded at least 3,000 borrowers to send their mortgage loan payments to a new address by informing them that their mortgages had been sold.

EQUITY LOANS HAVE STOLEN HOMES

If you own a home your mail will be filled with offers for preapproved equity loans because they have been snooping in your credit files.

These loans sound tempting because the only interest deductible on federal income tax is interest paid on mortgages. An equity loan can be used for almost anything. It can even be a "line of credit," which means you can write checks on it. It is always paid back as an additional mortgage on your home.

Most of these are scams.

For more than a quarter of a century, the California legislature has tried to scare off unscrupulous sales agents who peddle equity loans that require large fees and bloated interest rates. These aim to lead unsuspecting homeowners into losing their homes.

Other states, where property values are high, have the same problem with scam equity loans. In spite of all the laws that try to stop them, they seem to multiply faster than rabbits.

For instance: a widow nearly lost her home after taking out a $40,000 equity loan. All she intended to borrow was $2,000 to repair her car. But the smooth talkers convinced her a larger loan would be more to her benefit. The loan included $16,900 in loan fees and an interest rate of 26.15 percent. When she couldn't make her monthly $653 loan payment, they filed foreclosure proceedings against her home.

If you need an equity loan, go to a sound bank. A scam loan is designed to steal your home out from under you, or milk it for all its equity and then sell it at a foreclosure.

These very bad offers usually arrive in the mail, designed as a check already made out to you. Sometimes they arrive by telephone. If you find one in your mail, you should throw it in your garbage can as fast as you can. You will recognize such offers after opening one the first time, so don't open the envelopes again. Why tempt yourself? Better still, mark them refused and put them in your mailbox to be picked up by your mailman.

DON'T BE CONFUSED BY REVERSE MORTGAGES

These sound mortgages are entirely different. They are in their infancy and only at an experimental stage. The federal government now backs a certain amount of them.

Reverse mortgages make it possible for an older person to live comfortably by receiving a check each month that comes from the house equity. Instead of making mortgage payments, you get paid. Of course, some day someone must pay this money back, but usually not until the house sells or the owner dies, in which case it will come out of the sale money or estate.

The government does not solicit you to take out these reverse mortgages. Scam offers come to you in the mail. They are usually from a mortgage company that you never heard of. Seek a reputable mortgage firm.

TOWNHOUSES AND CONDOS

If you live in either of these, and should find construction problems in the future, be aware that some scabby builders are now forming collapsible corporations so that when they finish building, they fold and disappear. The owner then has nowhere to appeal.

- In Texas a developer cost banks and investors more than $200 million in one of the largest cases of title fraud in U.S. history. But he didn't do it alone. Investigations show that savings institutions fighting their way through a failing economy tried to bail out through the sweetheart deals he offered.

  They bought the "bargain" mortgages with high interest rates from the developer. The buildings contained many flaws. When the developer filed for bankruptcy, it was found that the properties were far over-appraised and worth 40 percent less than the banks and investors paid for them. The titles had been improperly transferred. They were still owned by the bankrupt developer.

- Similar frauds have occurred in Florida in the last few years.

If you consider buying a townhouse or a condominium, it is not enough to fall in love with the kitchen, the view, and the exercise room. Thoroughly investigate the homeowner's association related to the property. Ask your potential neighbors about the association. Demand a copy of the financial statement, the insurance policies and the rules and regulations of the association. Is it in good financial condition? Are the rules and regulations agreeable to you? Are the board members working as a cohesive group, or is there political in-fighting? Review the insurance policy on the home.

You will be charged a monthly fee for upkeep of the grounds, amenities (such as a swimming pool or meeting rooms) and the exterior of your home. If the association is not in good financial condition, necessary maintenance may suffer, or you may be charged an assessment which could amount to thousands of dollars.

If the association is not being well run, the officers, who will be your neighbors, may be battling around you about issues that will have an effect on your home's condition, appearance, resale value and not least, your peace of mind. Legal bills could eat up the association's assets and cost you a shocking amount of money.

STRAW BUYERS

This common fraud is a hard one to detect. In this scheme the "borrower" never intends to own the property. Instead, for a fee, the "borrower's" credit is used to qualify for the loan. After closing, a third party (often the seller or someone unable to qualify for the loan because of poor credit) assumes the loan.

Parents often buy homes for their children who have poor or no credit histories. Veterans sell their Veterans Administration (VA) entitlements.

NONASSUMED MORTGAGES

When the real estate market is off, sellers who are anxious to close a deal often don't use enough caution. One older couple, anxious to move to a retirement village, was having trouble selling their city condo. A young man offered to buy the condo by taking over their mortgage. Since they didn't have much equity, they were happy to be rid of the condo mortgage payments.

A year later they received a certified letter from the FHA notifying them that the condo was about to be sold at a foreclosure auction for nonpayment of the mortgage. To make matters worse, if the condo sold for less than the money owed, they would legally have to make up the difference!

A lawyer informed them they made the serious mistake of selling the condo subject to their mortgage without getting the buyer to assume their FHA mortgage. The assumption would have relieved them of further liability on the loan. As it was, there was nothing that could be done except hope that the auction price would cover the bill.

FLORIDA HIGH ON SCAMS

Florida still ranks high on the scale for land scams. Currently they are prosecuting a $300 million scam involving overpricing by over-appraisal of more than 10,000 homes. Another swindle involves homes built on 270,000 acres throughout the state.

GUARANTEED TIMESHARE RESALES

This potential scam affects Florida, Hawaii, and other warmer climes the most. People escaping from cold winters want to try out the area before making a permanent commitment or to await retirement, so they purchase a timeshare.

When they change their mind about the climate, move, or want to own something better, sellers of timeshare condominiums pay $300 to $400 to a resale agent, who guarantees a refund if the unit doesn't sell within a year. But the agent never makes good on the refund.

SAD STORIES

Josie's father died very suddenly. Her mother had Altzheimer's disease in the early stages. Josie and her husband moved her mother in to live with them and then they put her home on the market.

The real estate agent advised them to lower the price they expected and it sold the first day. When the final escrow papers arrived to be signed, they were puzzled. The name on the paper, under "buyer," was not the name they remembered the buyer using when they sold their house.

Josie couldn't put it out of her mind. She felt something had been put over on her and she was right. She went to the County Recorder's office and looked the sale up on the public microfilm files.

While her house was still in escrow for the too-low price recommended by the real estate man, the new owner had resold it for $18,000 more than Josie had originally wanted him to ask. The middle owner had thus made a profit of nearly $30,000 without ever living in the house or doing any improvements on it.

Just on a hunch she consulted other files at the County Registrar of Voters and Marriage Records and discovered the interim buyer had been the real estate salesman's married daughter.

She hired a real estate attorney to sue for the $30,000 that should have rightly gone to her and reported the matter to the state real estate commissioner. The man lost his real estate license. Her civil case is still pending.

Bea, depressed and lonely, wanted to live closer to her children after her divorce. She had a four-year-old townhouse but the market for townhouses was bad. After using two different real estate salespersons, she still had no offers.

The property was no longer listed when a young

man offered to buy her townhouse by taking over the mortgage.

Bea signed the papers and departed to a distant city. A year later she received a certified letter from the FHA notifying her that her townhouse was going up for foreclosure auction and she was going to be held liable for any loss that the FHA might suffer on her mortgage.

Her buyer had never made a mortgage payment. He had never lived in the townhouse but rented it out and skipped town with all the rent money.

A similar scheme was pulled on a couple in their 80s. A young man offered them their full asking price if they would let him buy subject to their existing first mortgage and accept a second mortgage for their equity. The buyer also paid their real estate fee.

It seemed like a good deal until six months later when they were informed their house was about to be wiped out at a foreclosure sale on the first mortgage. He, too, had been renting the house out and pocketing the rent money.

This is known as an "equity-skimming" scam. The elderly couple lacked any choice except to pay the first mortgage up to date and sue for the second mortgage — if the man can be found.

To protect yourself from some of these horrors, a good book to read is *Tips and Traps When Buying a Home*, by Robert Irwin, published by McGraw-Hill Publishing Co.

FOR COMPLAINTS ABOUT REAL ESTATE BROKERS AND AGENTS

- All real estate agents and brokers must be licensed by the state or states where they do business.
- Complaints can be filed with the state licensing or regulatory agency. This is usually the Real Estate Commission or the Department or Division of Real Estate.
- Contact your local consumer protection agency if you need help in contacting the licensing authority.
- Complaints about a realtor, a registered title limited to persons who are members of the National Association of Realtors, also may be taken to any of the 1800 local boards of realtors.
- These boards have standing grievance committees for handling consumer complaints.
- The National Association of Realtors is headquartered at 777 14th St. NW, Washington, DC 20005, (202) 383-1000

22

MOVING NIGHTMARES

Con games follow the seasons, the fads and the news. When a news story blamed the high cost of living as the reason so many retired people were relocating from their native cities — you guessed it: moving scams quickly fleeced many of them.

One such "mover" operated in different cities in the San Francisco Bay area from 1986 through 1989. It wasn't until more than 50 complaints poured in about his companies to police departments all over the area, that his many aliases tied together. To date his whereabouts is unknown.

Some goods he moved never arrived at their destination. In one case, $34,000 worth of silverware was missing. In cases where the furnishings came from affluent homes, he planned the arrival at the new destination so late that the truck had to be parked and unpacked the next morning to give himself the opportunity to remove items of value.

The scam mover would quote a low estimate over the phone. When he was ready to unload, the price had always risen $300 or $400. He claimed the client had misrepresented the load, or added things at the last minute.

In effect, he held people and their possessions

hostage. He would not unload their property until they came up with the money.

An investigation by the California Public Utilities Commission found he had several driver's licenses under assumed names. He also had ten places of business and advertised his moving business under ten different names in the Yellow Pages of ten different cities. All the ads had false licensing numbers.

He has skipped from California. Most likely he is operating somewhere else in the country under a new name — or ten.

Don't be penny wise and pound foolish! Scam movers have disappeared with entire van loads of furniture. They always offer you very low estimates. But when — and if — your shipment arrives at your new home, there is always a large extra bill for $300 or $400 or more that must be paid before they will unpack.

As anyone who has ever moved knows, when that truck arrives at your new home with your belongings, your brain is almost mush and your body is screaming "Let's get this over with!"

So you pay and resolve to complain about this to authorities when you are settled. By then you probably can not locate the mover.

SELECTING A MOVER

Call your friends to find what movers they used and with what results. Call the accounting department of a large corporation and ask a secretary who her company hires to move its employees around the country. Seek out a moving firm that has been in the business for a dozen or more years.

If you begin your search for a mover through the Yellow Pages, look at the corners of the ad. On the left will be the firm's state license number. On the right will you will see an ICC number. This is their Interstate Commerce license. Make a note of these numbers.

Find out if there have been any complaints against this company. You can do this by checking with:

- The Better Business Bureau
- The Bureau of Consumer Affairs
- The Police Bunco Squad if necessary
- Your local library. Use their data research computer and microfilm machines to search through back issues of newspapers.
- Your local newspaper also keeps files on microfilm. Someone has the information you need before your possessions go onto a truck. Do it early before you are exhausted and confused with the many little things you must remember.

If the company comes up clean, they are most likely a reliable family-owned small moving company. They are often a good bargain.

A SAFE MOVE

If you must watch your dollars, and you are shipping your household goods with a somewhat unknown mover, but driving your car or cars to the new destination, plan to carry your jewelry, silverware and most important documents with you. Devise a way of concealing them in your vehicle.

Don't leave them in your car unattended while you sleep in a hotel or motel. When you do stop to eat, park just outside a window and sit at a table where your car is in view.

If you possess very new or antique furniture, or have cared for your possessions so that they still are without scratches and mars, take colored photos of them from several different angles and date them. Many photo developers date the prints as they make them.

For insurance purposes it is a good idea to photograph every room in your house and its contents. (These photos also will come in handy if you ever suffer a fire or burglary.)

With most of the moving companies who are very reliable and have been in business for many years, this may prove to be unnecessary. But there is always the exception when you will be glad that you did.

Be observant while your possessions are loaded. Every moving company lists each item on a loading manifest as the item goes into the truck. This list comes in different colors to assist the driver in identifying one household from another, as large vans often carry more than one shipment. Everything tagged blue, for instance, will be yours.

This list describes the condition of each piece as

it goes on the van. Even if the scratch is tiny, the well-polished dining room table may be listed as "marred." If a large new scratch appears during the unpacking, the mover's insurance will go by the written note "marred before loaded." This is when you will appreciate the photographs you took.

Check the manifest before the moving van leaves your home. Have they listed everything? If something is missing upon arrival at the new destination, their insurance will not accept your word that it was loaded, or even existed.

It is at this point that moving companies claim that, while they are not trying to scam the customer, the customer often tries to scam them. At the time the moving company inspects your possessions, their representative gives you a "binding estimate" that states how much your move will cost.

In California all movers, upon writing a binding estimate, must give the customers a pamphlet, *Important Information for Shippers of Used Household Goods in California.* It offers information to avoid problems with the mover, or loss or damage to property. Other states also follow this practice.

But this binding estimate can be raised when the van reaches the weighing station. This is because, intentionally or unintentionally, the customer has included additional items.

In preparation for this, many people will get extra cash in advance so they can pay this extra charge when the van arrives at their new destination. This is not a scam.

At the time the movers load the van you must pay the amount listed on the binding estimate with a certified check or cash.

A reliable firm will include in the estimate an approximate time of arrival at the new destination. They will call you when they are an hour or two within the destination to give you the time of their arrival.

If traffic or weather problems have made them late, they will park the van in the yard of your new home, or somewhere nearby, and the driver will sleep in the van until morning. He will not leave your load unattended.

MOVING TALES

Throughout the Sun Belt states, because retired people favor them, moving company scams keep popping up.

Once in awhile, after you've paid the mover and rested before tackling all those boxes, you will find something wrong. Your furniture is badly scratched, your silverware is missing and the mover can't be located.

In one case a pair of con men used a stolen truck, painting a new name on it every week or so. Each time they chose expensive but the least obvious things to steal.

They can read your mind. They know your habits. They know that the first thing you want to do settle your bedroom so you can rest. The next thing, after a meal or two eaten out, is to tackle the kitchen and put it in order. The dining room or den is usually last.

So scammers keep an eye open on every item they load from these rooms. They appraise each item as they go and "forget" to write some of these plums down on the shipping manifest.

When you miss them, a) the mover is missing, or b) he has your signature for everything he loaded and unloaded, or c) "You were right there always watching, weren't you? Then you looked at the list and signed it right in front of me! What do you mean something is missing?"

He acts insulted, aggrieved, mumbles something about his attorney. You feel confused. You did watch him while he was loading because you didn't want anything marred or left behind. You did watch him unloading because you needed to tell him where to put each item.

"Then how come, folks, something is missing and you blame it on me?"

The con artist lacks a conscience, remember? The older people are, the more certain they are to be considerate and have a conscience. Are you going to stand there and make trouble for this poor hard-working man? Maybe you have just overlooked it and you will find it later. After all, there are still boxes to unpack.

But you remember: it wasn't put in a box. It was put in a drawer. You wrapped it in a thick bath towel and put it in a desk drawer to be safe. Later you emptied the desk drawer contents into a box to make room for the vases and statues. The man helped you, didn't he? Your head starts to ache. Did he help you or not?

He watches you. He sees you growing weak. "I saw you empty those drawers, Ma'am. But I was out of the room when you put something in them--*if* you put something in them."

Confusion! What to do? Headache. He leaves. "We'll talk about it on the phone tomorrow."

But his tomorrow never comes. Your missing articles never show up. You didn't notify your homeowner's insurance of your move yet. You are uncovered. You can't find him. You are up a creek.

MOVING INSURANCE

Call your homeowner's insurance carrier as soon as you plan a move. Ask for an *in-transit* policy, and also for immediate coverage upon arrival at your new home.

23

STEALING YOUR CREDIT

The use of bank credit cards has made life easier for almost all of us, *especially the professional thief.*

The losses from credit card fraud from 1980 to 1990 were close to $1.5 billion. But credit card scams were mostly just pilfering in those years. The most daring, large-scale thefts occurred during 1990.

Many people own more than one type of card. Some people make active use of five or six cards. This makes it very hard for some cardholders to keep track of all their cards and purchases.

In an attempt to foil forgers, some credit card issuers are using holographs (which cannot yet be forged) on the face of the cards. To forge a card, the thief first has to steal someone's account number.

THE FRANCHISED TELEMARKETING/ POSTCARD SCHEME

The most recent and perhaps the worst credit card scam has prompted legislation in at least four states. Postcard or telephone solicitations promise Visa or MasterCard cards with low interest rates, no fees, and $5000 credit lines. They charge from $98 to $200 for giving information about banks which make these cards available. All the victim gets, however, is a short list of several banks offering lower-than average rates — banks which have not authorized the marketers to guarantee or even to market their credit cards.

Consumers pay huge amounts for this information, available at little or no cost from banks, newspapers and magazines, and from Bankcard Holders of America as well as other consumer advocacy groups.

Although it has been discovered that only a handful of companies have been the main ringleaders behind these boiler room setups, they have actually "franchised" this marketing scheme to many small operators throughout the country.

In other telemarketing schemes related to credit card offers, the victim is asked to give information over the telephone in order to qualify: credit card numbers from his other accounts, bank account numbers and other important information which makes it possible to steal his credit.

COUNTLESS SMALLER OPERATIONS

Among the many reports of credit card scams, one recently read of a forger who duplicated bank credit cards. Before he was caught, he made off with $50,000.

Automatic teller machine cards are also forged. On one weekend, a man attempted to clean out a bank with forged cards.

Two teenage boys managed to spend nearly

$100,000 on a wild spree with stolen credit cards. They hired a private plane, visited several tropical resorts, and lived in high style.

THE METHODS THEY USE

One way credit thieves obtain stolen credit card account numbers is from trash cans, where carbon copies of sales receipts are tossed. Telephone purchases can be made with the account numbers, or the numbers can be duplicated on forged cards and used or sold.

To protect their customers, many stores are now using credit card sales receipts that require no carbon copies.

But plug up one river and thieves always find another channel. A tapped mail order phone line is a gold mine. Remember if you are using a cordless phone, anyone with a radio in his car can easily eavesdrop. Or if you give your credit card number over your car phone to a hotel reservation clerk, a nearby car can listen in and get your number. And they don't actually have to be too close!

ELECTRONIC THIEVES

Once a thief with a desk-top computer gets your credit card information, it can be posted on a computer "bulletin board," where it can be used by anyone who has access to a simple computer system. There it can be read by any computer with a modem, a telephone link to any telephone in the world. Members who subscribe to that bulletin board, which is like a television newspaper, can buy, trade for, or copy the stolen number.

The bulletin board call-ins can post the number all over the country so purchases occur in dozens of different areas simultaneously. This gives them time to purchase and disappear. The only thing to stop them is your credit limit.

They can even get around that by shopping from widely different areas in the country at shops that check credit cards manually instead of using an electronic system. These merchants only know if your card is still active. Your credit limit can be used limitless times in this manner.

Bank credit card companies urge merchants to install electronic systems for checking, or to telephone in for an okay in an attempt to shrink the gap between the time you make purchases and when they are recorded to hold down losses.

The minute the crime is discovered and the credit card number canceled, these hackers seem to learn about it, too. Then they send out the warning over the same linkage so everyone can go under cover or scatter.

YOUR LIABILITY

Imagine this scenario. You receive an outrageous inaccurate credit card statement. It shows your account billed up to its limit. You are planning a long trip. Now your credit is a mess. You must spend time and headaches to untangle it.

- You must write the card issuer promptly to report any questionable charges. Written inquiries should not be included with your payment. Instead, check the billing statement for the correct address for billing questions. The inquiry must be in writing and *must be sent within 60 days* to guarantee your rights under the Fair Credit Billing Act.

- If any of your credit cards are missing or stolen, report the loss at once to the card issuer. Check your credit card statement for a telephone number for reporting stolen credit cards. Follow up your phone calls with a letter to each card issuer. The letter should contain your card number, the date the cards were missing, and the date you called in the loss.

- *If you report the loss before a credit card is used*, the issuer cannot hold you responsible for any subsequent unauthorized charges. If a thief uses your card before you report it missing, the most you will owe for unauthorized charges on each card is $50.

- It can take from a month to two months to discover all the illegal charges on your account. It is best to get a new card with a new account number to let this old account die. You will still have to prove that you didn't make the charges on the old account. Sometimes your charges arrive a month or two late.

- In general you are not liable for fraudulent mail-order bills because you may not even know someone has stolen your number. These fraudulent charges can mess up your credit history until they are resolved. *You must prove them to be illegal orders.*

PRECAUTIONS

If you live in the State of California there are some new rules in effect to protect credit card users. Merchants can be fined $250 for asking shoppers to provide a credit card number when paying by check. Merchants may only ask to see your credit cards as long as they don't copy down the account number.

Another piece of legislation prohibits merchants from demanding your address or phone number for a credit card purchase. Merchants who ask for the information can be fined from $250 to $1,000.

If you live in other parts of the country, similar legislation may be in effect or being planned. Write or call your local legislative representative.

- Always keep your credit card numbers where you can locate them and call them in to the bank if you miss the cards. Your purse or wallet is not a good place.
- When using a credit card, keep track of it. Be sure the clerk hands it back to you.
- Never sign a blank receipt. Draw a line through any blank spaces above the total

when you sign receipts.

- Open your credit card bills promptly and compare them with your receipts to check for unauthorized charges and billing errors.
- Never give your credit card number over the telephone unless you made the call. Better yet, mail a check instead of charging over the telephone.
- Sign new cards when they arrive. Cut up the old ones. Discard in a small paper bag or envelope tucked in the garbage or trash.
- When you shop always ask for the carbon copies of your transaction. Tear them up and discard them at home, not in public trash.
- It is safer to use only one or two credit cards. Always know where they, and keep track of all your receipts and carbons. The best system is to file them at home as you do your canceled checks. These receipts could even help you at income tax time. Why aid a thief?
- Avoid one-shot credit cards that are always being offered to you in the mail. Those who have no credit, but want to establish credit, are the target for these cards. The cards cost $35 to $50 per year but can be used only to buy products from the card issuer's catalog. A comparison of these prices with other catalogs proves the prices to be greatly inflated.
- For useful information about credit cards,

write to:

Bankcard Holders of America
560 Herndon Parkway, Suite 120
Herndon, VA 22070
(703) 481-1110

This nonprofit consumer education agency offers pamphlets such as *Traveling With Your Credit Card, Consumer Rights Under Federal Law, How to Choose a Credit Card,* and *Managing Family Debt.*

24

TRAPS THAT ARRIVE IN THE MAIL

Letters that are scams often arrive in official-looking envelopes. The return address may be only a letter or two away from a real name of a government agency. These letters usually urge you to call an 800 telephone number. They always say that they have some urgent vital information that you need. When you do call, you'll be invited to pay for information you can get elsewhere for free.

The most frequent ones that are making the current rounds are official-appearing checks that purport to be the first payment on an equity loan on your house that has already been cleared for acceptance. Don't cash it! Feed it to a billy goat!

Last year consumers spent more than $90 billion on mail-order merchandise. An estimated 1 percent of that, or more than $900 million, was wasted on frauds. Mail order problems rank among the most often heard by Better Business Bureaus and state consumer protection officials.

CLASSIC MAIL CONS

- *Sweepstakes swindles.* You are told you have won a prize but you must pay a "redemption fee" or "shipping costs" or if it is a loose gem, a "mounting fee."

- *Charity frauds.* These charities usually benefit no one but the promoters.

- *Chain letters.* You receive a letter asking you to send $50 to someone and add your name to the list to receive many times $50. This is illegal. There is no way anyone can win except the people at the top of the list — who wrote to you.

- *Work-at-home schemes.* Shut-ins, children, the elderly and the handicapped are often lured by ads for "profitable work that can be done at home." You are asked to send $5 or $10 for "information," or perhaps a "sales kit."

- *Medical quackery.* Millions of dollars are wasted on anti-aging formulas, sex nutrients, cancer cures, bust developers. None work. Some are dangerous.

- *Lucky charms.* A small fortune is spent every year on these!

- *The empty warehouse.* One of the quickest ways to defraud is to advertise something everyone wants, offer it at a reduced price, and ship nothing because you have nothing.

Scams work because dissatisfied customers don't complain. They usually keep prices modest so customers can shrug off their losses. Even legitimate businesses hear from only 4 percent of dissatisfied customers.

Once you have bought some fraudulent item by mail order, you can expect to get more offers — you'll land on a "sucker" list.

The U.S. Postal Service uses more than 300 Postal Service inspectors working full-time to investigate about 4,000 civil and criminal cases a year. It prosecutes nearly 2000 a year and wins about 98 percent of them. But new ones keep originating.

MAIL ORDER SCAM BUSINESSES

One company sells mostly smut under seemingly familiar titles: The Digest, U.S. Geographic Society, U.S. Map and Atlas Co., Webster Dictionary Co. — to confuse buyers with Reader's Digest, National Geographic Magazine, Webster's Dictionary.

Another company sells useless novelty and household items listed as kerosene lamps, ceiling fans, air conditioners, cookware, china, medical products such as diet and sex pills. Example: "world's smallest air conditioner" for $11 consists of a plastic box about two inches square with a plastic fan inside and two "wet" pads. No cooling effect at all. They sold 155,000 of these fakes.

A direct marketing firm sells worthless jewelry, among other items. Best known for its emeralds, pearls and diamonds. The emeralds, ($4 plus $2 for handling) are cloudy, filled with black streaks, and badly cut. They are worth about 20 to 50 cents at most. They are the road gravel from emerald mines. Estimated sales — $104 million.

Another busy outfit sells diet pills, tarpaulins,

binoculars, electronic muscle stimulators and other products. Best known for its "sea and field binoculars with 50-mile range — only $9 a pair" (plastic toy binoculars). They sold 1.5 million of these useless binoculars.

HOW TO PROTECT YOURSELF

- Read advertisements carefully and completely, especially the small print. Don't rely on pictures and headlines.
- Never send cash. Pay by check, money order, or credit card so you have receipt of payment.
- Don't send for a product from a company you're not familiar with if the advertisement lists only a post office box.
- Be wary of companies that require the use of toll-free 800 numbers and charge cards. This may be an attempt to get around using the mails and federal postal statutes.
- Keep all advertisements, envelopes and correspondence with a company in case you have complaints about your order. (Some firms require that you send in the original ad with your order. In that case, copy the ad before you send it in.)
- If you order by phone, keep a record of the original price, date, time of your conversation and the name of the person you spoke with.

After you order you have certain rights. The merchandise must reach you within 30 days of the company receiving your order (your canceled check will give you that date on its back). If the seller can't process your order in time they must send you a letter stating when you will receive it. It must contain a stamped self-addressed envelope to give you a chance to cancel the order.

If you cancel, the company must mail you a refund within seven business days if you paid by check or money order. If you paid by credit card, it must credit your account within one billing cycle (one month).

Remember that any scheme that makes use of the mails, however remotely, even if it's just sending your check to the gypster, can fall within the jurisdiction of the Chief Postal Inspector. Send suspect material to:

Chief Postal Inspector
U.S. Post Office Department
Washington, DC 20260

All so-called junk mail is not associated with scams and fraud. But if you want the delivery of junk mail stopped, you can write to:

Mail Preference Service
Direct Marketing Association
6 E. 43rd St.
P.O. Box 3861
Grand Central Station
New York, NY 10163-3861

This is a trade organization that compiles a delete file to send its members every three months. They will see to it that your name and address is no longer sold to mailing lists.

No one is obligated to remove your name from these lists, but some report they do because it's just good business. Mail addressed to "Occupant" can't be stopped.

MAIL ORDER SCAM

Larry saw a hobby magazine ad for a real bargain on an item he had long wanted. With time now to pursue his hobby with enthusiasm, he didn't hesitate to mail a $50 check which included postage and handling. The magazine was one he'd read for years. He had purchased other things from their ads. He assumed they screened their advertisers. He was wrong.

After waiting a month for the item, it arrived by UPS a few days after Christmas. When he opened it, he saw, without even removing it from the box, that it was broken, and judging from the amount of packing material, it must have been broken before it was shipped. It also didn't appear to be new merchandise.

There was a slip in the box that said, "We cannot accept returns more than seven days after they are shipped." The UPS label did not show the date it was shipped. In fact the label was smeared so badly he could hardly read it.

He had to find the magazine ad to look up the address. There was a phone number in case you wished to use MasterCard or Visa. So he called them.

"Sorry," they said. "This number is only to be used when ordering merchandise by MasterCard or Visa."

"But the merchandise arrived broken."

"We make no exceptions. You had seven days to return it. We have it printed right on the warranty slip."

"It didn't arrive until today."

"Our records show we shipped all of that merchandise 14 days ago."

"But you mailed it during the height of the Christmas rush!"

"Sorry. We make no exceptions. You could have read that in the fine print in the ad."

"But if you had mailed it when you received my check it would have arrived before the Christmas rush."

"We process as fast as we can. We make no exceptions."

While he was talking he had very carefully removed the item from the box and examined it. "Also, it is not only broken, but it looks like it has been used — and not just a little."

"Sir! All of our merchandise is not only new, but inspected for flaws before we send it out. There is nothing we can do for you!" They hung up on him.

He looked through the pile of Christmas mail that had stacked up in the last week and found the statement and the canceled check. The company had cashed the check on December 2nd. So he returned the item with a letter of explanation.

Days later the package came back to him unopened.

Larry called the Better Business Bureau in Columbus, Ohio.

They replied, "Yes, we've had more than two dozen similar complaints against the company in the past month. We've driven out there. They were apparently working out of a vacant garage of a house that was for rent. There is no one there now. The police are investigating it."

Could Larry have saved himself from this scam? Yes. He had been wanting that particular item for quite sometime and had looked at it in stores. He was trapped because the ad listed it for less than half the regular retail price he had seen in discount stores. He had forgotten the old adage of how not to get stung: *If it appears too good to be true — it most likely is not true!*

SWEEPSTAKES WINNER

Lou was aware that mailing lists abound that listed her by her credit listing, affluence, and area of residence. So when she received a check for 10 cents in the mail, she laughed and read on for the sting.

She wasn't surprised to learn that she was a lucky winner of a sweepstakes, "But this is a charity event to raise money for the Cancer Fund. To find out which of these listed prizes you have won, you must first mail us $5 for the Cancer Fund."

She laughed all the way to the bank where she deposited the 10-cent check.

"For an investment of 35 cents they thought they could con me out of $5! Now let them handle this 10 cents on their books!"

She turned in all the enclosed literature to the Postmaster. "I just wonder how many kind souls did send them $5 or more?"

"Too many," he sighed. He forwarded her evidence to the investigators.

THE WINNER!

Catherine "won" a Caribbean cruise. "All expenses paid except port taxes, airline taxes, hotel taxes. Please forward us $200 to cover these minor things and tell us which dates you prefer to travel and which of these deluxe hotels you wish to use for your three nights ashore. Your tickets will be air expressed as soon as your check clears."

Catherine photocopied everything and mailed it to her friend, the editor of a magazine. He wrote back, "I'm sorry to tell you, it's a scam. I hope you aren't too disappointed." She turned hers over to the postal investigators, also.

All of these incidents I have mentioned are federal criminal offenses and will be prosecuted when the culprits are caught. The more people who turn this kind of mail into the Postal Service, the sooner the investigations can start.

C.O.D. TRAPS

Walter was still stumbling around in shock over the loss of his wife. She'd been his jewel — one who paid all the bills, managed all the mundane things in life, sheltered him from intrusions to leave him time to work on his scientific research.

When the man came to the door and said "C.O.D. for Mrs. . ." Walter didn't hesitate to sign for it.

"It's heavy," he said.

"She must think a lot of you," the man said as Walter signed with a trembling hand. "This is some kind of special gift for you — 24 karat gold plated. Your birthday?"

"No." Walter went for the checkbook he had seen on her desk.

"No checks!" the delivery man said. "I'm only allowed to accept cash. That's $425.95."

"Well, you're in luck. I cashed a royalty check for $500 just two hours ago." He handed the money over to the man who left in a rush. Walter sat down and reverently opened what seemed to him like a final farewell gift. The box contained nothing but newspapers and beach sand.

Shocked, he collapsed in a chair, then remembered the conversation he'd had at the crowded bank on the corner. The teller had commiserated with him on the loss of his wife and congratulated him on the royalty check while she cashed it for him.

His scam was never solved. He learned how to use

electronic banking and to have a trusted son cosign his checks. He also learned to never discuss his private affairs when there are strangers within earshot.

This scam is an old one. As old as the Pony Express, ships carrying mail from Europe to the new colonies, and probably carried out under the eyes of the Sphinx. Where and whenever it has been possible to collect on delivery, someone has figured out a scam.

The easiest targets, of course, are the bereaved; the old and fragile who think and react slowly; the lonely who are always hoping to receive something from someone; and the vain who think they are too smart to be fooled, so they are careless. All of these victims are carefully selected. The bereaved are frequently located through newspaper obituaries and silently observed to find their plucking point.

If you haven't ordered something, refuse to accept a C.O.D.

Another pointer on C.O.Ds: never accept — or pay for — a C.O.D. package for a neighbor. There's a very good chance your neighbor didn't order anything. It is against the law to ask for payment for items never ordered!

FIGHT BACK!

If you have been skinned in any kind of mail fraud, it's probably too late to get your money back. But there's always a chance that the perpetrator can be taken out of circulation for a while and that others can be warned. Here are the agencies you can contact:

Chief Postal Inspector
U.S. Post Office Department
Washington, DC 20260

Or the nearest postal inspector. Any scheme that makes use of the mails, however remotely, even if it's just sending your check to the gypster can all be within his or her jurisdiction.

Food and Drug Administration
Department of Health, Education
and Welfare
Washington, DC 20201

This agency is concerned with medicines, medical devices and equipment advertised or shipped through the mails.

Federal Trade Commission
Washington, DC 20580

The Federal Trade Commission handles complains involving false or misleading advertising, misbranding and unfair competition.

25

CLASSIC CONS STILL WORK!

"Monte" may be the oldest "sucker game" in the world. There are indications that it was played in ancient Egypt. It was played on the old Mississippi River boats. It is played on Wall Street on the sidewalks during lunch time. And the game has never changed. The "team" always wins and the suckers always lose.

It has been known by different names. Sometimes it's played with a pea under walnut shell halves — sound familiar? Then it is called the *shell game*. Usually it is played with a little ball and caps.

If you've played it, you've never been able to figure out how you lost every time you watched so closely! You were sure you knew which shell the pea was under, but it never was. You felt determined that you would win the next round. But sorry, you lost again.

In New York City in the financial district during lunch time there are never less than five games going and it takes a team of five men to run against the suckers. The same occurs in almost every big city, beach resort, carnival, fair, rodeo — wherever crowds gather.

The secret of the game is not in the pea or the ball or your observation skills, it lies in the rapid patter of the *shaker*. It may sound like just rattling but every bit of it is rapid fire instructions to his other four team members — the two *sticks* sometimes called *shills* who place bets and win to keep the victims excited, and the *slides* who stand back-to-back just a few feet back from the crowd watching for the police and the undercover detectives. They can spot them in an instant. They shout the secret word and the game folds and readjourns at a different spot.

A good team easily cons $1,500 a day, and that is only five men working a few hours. Suckers love to be taken by con men.

In that rapid patter of the shaker, a clue word is "open," which instructs his slides to open up to make room for *marks* to move in. "Close" means to close them into the table. The sticks make all kinds of happy, disgusted, argumentative conversation with the shaker to pretend that they are really winning and losing.

By the way, in the modern game, there are no peas or shells; too much effort to get them. The cons steal the caps off liter soft drink bottles at drug stores and use cakes of rouge which they carve into the little balls. The tables are cardboard boxes that they dig out of the trash. They don't believe in overhead, only pure profit.

This is just one of the most common con games, running all the time, somewhere. But the others, equally old, are also still working fine. Con artists are actors with a constantly moving stage and their paying customers don't have to buy reserved seats. The actors take them wherever they find them.

EVERY CON GAME REQUIRES THREE ELEMENTS TO SUCCEED

- The approach: conversation is made to determine if the victim will stop to listen to the pitch or if the victim has enough money to make the theft worthwhile.

- The "benefit": it has to look like the victim is going to get something for nothing. Or else it has to be based on superstition. That's why for centuries gypsy fortune tellers have been so successful.

- The money: the con must find a way to make the victim actually show his or her money. Once the money is in sight, various ways are used to relieve the sucker of it, but the most common is switching of envelopes, wallets, handkerchiefs or other personal effects.

THE PIGEON DROP

This one is so old you would hardly believe it could still work, but it does. The victim is a person — usually an elderly woman — leaving her home, in a department store, entering or leaving a public place, or entering or leaving a bank. One member of a two-person team approaches the victim and starts a conversation of any sort with her. The second person runs up, very excited, with a "newly found package" of money of an unknown value.

There is an excited conversation over how to divide it, and they offer to share it with the victim if she will put up "good faith money." Surprisingly, people will draw large amounts of money from their banks and hand it over to a stranger in exchange for a package of newspaper.

Sometimes the pigeon drop has a slight switch. Instead of a package, there may be a wallet. There will be a card in the wallet. Or the wallet will contain "rare coins." For some reason the finder can't call the wallet's owner, but has the victim call the name on the card (usually a doctor), who offers a big reward for the return of his wallet. Again, the victim must put up "good faith money" before she goes to collect the reward, only to find that no such doctor or address exists.

THE BANK EXAMINER FRAUD

A team arrives in town and begins making telephone calls, saying they are bank examiners and that they need to check out the honesty of one of their employees. They ask the victim to cooperate by withdrawing a certain sum (usually $10,000) from his or (usually) her account as a test.

"A bank associate will arrive at your home, show you his police badge, take you to the bank to pick up the money, and then check to see if the employee recorded it. After the test the money will be put back into your account without any loss of interest."

False! You will never see that money again. Banks do not send bank examiners to your home to take you to the bank to pick up money!

The phoney bank examiners will either drive the victim to the bank or hire a cab. This is so they can observe if the victim is having any trouble with the real bank staff when she makes the withdrawl. If there is any hesitation by the teller, they scram.

Avoid becoming a victim:

- Don't discuss your personal finances with strangers.

- Don't draw cash out at the suggestion of someone you don't know. Remember: no legitimate bank examiner or officer or law enforcement official would ever call you by phone or visit you at home to ask your participation in this type of investigation. If you get such a call or visit, call your local police or district attorney's fraud unit.

- Don't believe that a person is an "official" without first checking with the agency the person — man or woman — supposedly works for.

- Don't get involved in anything where you are asked to demonstrate "good faith" or money resources.

- Don't expect to get something for nothing, especially from strangers on the street or phone.

- Don't let strangers in your house.

HOME INVASION TRICKS

Vagabond thieves use a number of tricks to gain entry into homes: they may say they sell magazine subscriptions; they may ask directions; they may feign illness.

Once they gain entry, they make excuses to get into other parts of the house. One of the thieves may ask to use the restroom or telephone, or ask for a drink of water. While the other thief keeps the attention of the victim, the thief using the restroom or telephone or getting a drink of water searches the house for valuables, money, or jewelry. Then they leave.

Thieves may also try to gain access to a victim's home by posing as utility repairmen or as home insulation inspectors who may offer a free inspection. They flash a card very quickly at the victim, who thinks the card is official identification and allows them to enter.

To avoid being a victim of an invasion trick:

- Insist on seeing the identification card of anyone who claims to be a serviceman representing some type of utility such as gas and electric, water department or the telephone company.
- Be especially wary of a person claiming to be an inspector who appears without your

request or who claims to be looking for a gas leak.

- If still in doubt, look up the name of the company in the phone book. Call to verify if it sent someone out.

BE AWARE!

The world is full of good guys and bad guys. You can never afford to let your guard down. Always know with whom you are confiding. Strangers cannot be trusted. Don't just trust to luck that you will meet one who can.

- If anyone offers you any kind of a deal and it sounds too good to be true, it probably isn't true.

- Nobody gives you something for nothing. So throw away the "sweepstakes" offers that come in the mail, the "free gift offers" and the bargain travel gifts, unopened, or return them to the sender if there is a self-addressed, no postage required envelope enclosed. Throw the outside envelope away or fold it inside. That will tell them to leave you alone! It will also usually remove you from their junk mail list.

- If a con artist looked or acted crooked he or she wouldn't be successful. These people are often attractive and sympathetic. It's by pretending to be interested in you and your problems and being sympathetic that they bore their way into your life. That's why they are called *confidence* men or women.

- Beware of the *tear-jerker*, the person who claims he needs help because he lost his wallet, or his ticket, and asks you for money. Common at airports.

- Swindles grow out of whatever is current in the headlines, such as earthquakes, floods, or fire relief frauds. Criminals prey on our carelessness when we overlook important details and precautions.

- Never be so foolish as to think that you know everything that you ever need to know. Con artists know how to read your type!